NAMIBIAN INDEPENDENCE:
A GLOBAL RESPONSIBILITY

To the memory of Srimathi Indira Gandhi
 A devoted friend of the people of Namibia
 and the Non-Aligned Movement

NAMIBIAN INDEPENDENCE

A Global Responsibility

A. W. SINGHAM
SHIRLEY HUNE

Lawrence Hill & Company

WESTPORT, CONNECTICUT

Published in the United States of America
by Lawrence Hill and Company, Publishers, Inc.
520 Riverside Avenue, Westport, Connecticut
06880

Library of Congress Cataloging-in-Publication Data

Singham, A. W.
    Namibian independence.

    Bibliography: p. 103
    1. Namibia—History—Autonomy and independence
movements. 2. Namibia—Politics and government—
1946-   . 3. Namibia—Foreign relations—Developing
countries. 4. Developing countries—Foreign relations—
Namibia. 5. United Nations—Namibia. I. Hune, Shirley.
II. Title.
DT714.S57 1985   968.8'03   85-21916
ISBN 0-88208-206-X (pbk.)

    1 2 3 4 5 6 7 8 9

Printed in the United States of America

Contents

ACKNOWLEDGMENTS

The authors wish to thank the officials and countries of the Non-Aligned Movement, especially those who opened doors at the various gatherings. The government of Algeria offered us hospitality and research assistance in Algiers during the extraordinary meeting. The UN Council for Namibia and the Secretariat provided considerable assistance, especially at the International Conference in Paris. The Center for Research in Rural and Industrial Development in Chandigarh knows how much we treasure our association with them. A special word of thanks to our Black brothers and sisters in the United States who shared our concerns and listened to innumerable talks, lectures, and sermons on Namibia. In addition, we would like to thank Shanti Assefa for her assistance in compiling the Select Bibliography. Finally, the greatest support came from SWAPO, "the sole and authentic representative of the people of Namibia," who are engaged in a heroic struggle against a most formidable opponent.

1: Introduction: Namibia— Sacred Trust of the International Community

Namibia's independence has always been a concern of the international community. Designated South West Africa, it was a German colony from 1884 until World War I. After Germany's defeat in 1918, the territory became a responsibility of the new League of Nations. Under the Covenant of the League, colonies and territories, such as South West Africa, "which as a consequence of the late war have ceased to be under the sovereignty of the States which formerly governed them, and which are inhabited by peoples not yet able to stand by themselves under the strenuous conditions of the modern world," were to have applied to them "the principal that the well-being and development of such peoples form a sacred trust of civilization and that securities for the performance of this trust should be embodied in this Covenant."

During the war, the territory had been invaded and occupied by its neighbor, the Republic of South Africa. With the defeat of Germany, the League of Nations mandated the territory to South Africa in 1920 under the category of "C" status, in which South Africa was expected to "promote to the utmost the material and moral well-being and social progress of the inhabitants of the territory." To the contrary, the government of South Africa has to this day pursued a policy of exploitation and annexation of the territory. Its aim of colonization was revealed after the dissolution of the League of Nations and the formation of the United Nations in 1945. South Africa refused to transfer the League mandate to the UN Trusteeship Council as outlined in the UN Charter—a charter signed by South Africa—even after the International Court of Justice in an advisory opinion in 1950 found the territory to be still under international mandate requiring South Africa to follow international obligations. Furthermore, at the first session of the United Nations General Assembly in 1946, South Africa requested that the territory be incorporated into its Union. Upon the refusal of the General Assembly to accede to this request, the South African government declared it would administer the territory without UN jurisdiction and shortly afterward began introducing its apartheid system there. In 1971, the International Court of Justice declared South Africa in illegal occupation of Namibia, but to this date it has retained control of Namibia, treating the territory and its inhabitants essentially as a part of the Republic of South Africa.

For over one hundred years the people of Namibia have been the victims of the politics of postponement. Their occupation, their colonization, and their exploitation have been duly documented and widely publicized. Yet while nearly all the colonies of the world have won their independence, Namibia remains a colony, with its future intertwined in the vicissitudes of global and regional power politics. The people of Namibia have persevered in their struggle for self-determination while South Africa has delayed. In 1960, the Namibian people founded the South West Africa People's Organization (SWAPO) to co-ordinate their independence movement. By 1966, as their efforts for a diplomatic solution were being ignored, SWAPO undertook the gigantic task of armed struggle against South Africa in order to gain Namibia's independence. To have engaged one of the world's most powerful and modern military machines for so long and to force that power along with its allies to come to the negotiating table represents a major military and diplomatic victory for a liberation movement. SWAPO has followed the pattern of other liberation movements for self-determination, such as Algeria, Vietnam, Angola, Mozambique, and Zimbabwe.

Over the years, the international community has sought South

Africa's co-operation in obtaining Namibia's independence, but has been faced with that government's refusal to negotiate with the United Nations in good faith. South Africa had hoped that the world would forget about Namibia. The global community, however, cannot forget its "sacred trust" of Namibia. The Namibian people have continuously and persistently taken their plight to the United Nations and built up a global consensus for their liberation struggle. SWAPO has the regional support of the front-line states of southern Africa, the continental support of the Organization of African Unity (OAU), and the international support of the Non-Aligned Movement (NAM). Over the years, these groupings have given direct moral and material aid to the Namibian people. Most important, they have also worked within the United Nations to achieve Namibia's independence. This issue has gained the broad support of the international community. As a result, the United Nations revoked South Africa's mandate in 1966, assumed in principle the administration of Namibia through the UN Council for Namibia (originally named the UN Council for South West Africa), and recognized SWAPO in 1973 as the "sole and authentic representative of the people of Namibia." This internationalization of the question of Namibia's independence plays an important role in supporting the struggle of the Namibian people and SWAPO. Although progress has been made, still Namibia is not free.

A great deal has already been written about the role of the United Nations in insuring that Namibian independence is obtained as soon as possible. The study begins with a brief chronology of the major events and decisions within the UN system in support of Namibian independence. But the question remains: Why has Namibia's independence been postponed and what can be done to accelerate the process? On the issue of independence the entire family of nations is ostensibly in agreement, including the United States, whose Reagan administration has entered into a policy of "constructive engagement" with the South African government. Still, this lone nation, the Republic of South Africa, has been able to defy the global community and continues to subjugate the people of Namibia.

No international grouping has played as significant a role in supporting the rights of the Namibian people and in promoting the independence of Namibia as the Non-Aligned Movement. The purpose of this study is to examine the role of the NAM in advancing the issue of Namibia's independence at the United Nations and in building international support and solidarity at a time when it was unpopular to call for Namibia's independence. The NAM was critical in galvanizing the global consensus around UN Security Council resolution 435. In 1978, the UN accepted the offer of a group of Western countries to lend their diplomatic efforts to facilitate the negotiations settlement with South Africa. The study considers how the Contact Group, led by the United States in collaboration with South Africa, has attempted to hijack the Namibian issue outside of the UN system and to make it part and parcel of the new Cold War. It also considers how their introduction of new elements into the negotiations process has complicated the UN settlement plan and benefitted South Africa. We offer explanations of how South Africa has been able to manipulate existing contradictions in world politics, notably, the new Cold War, to postpone Namibia's independence. Thus, in spite of the efforts of the Namibian people and SWAPO, the front-line states, the Organization of African Unity, the Non-Aligned Movement, and the United Nations, the negotiations process was derailed by the Contact group.

What was primarily a peaceful multilateral process under the auspices of the United Nations has been gradually transformed into a confrontational bilateral impasse, with the United States and South Africa acting as a joint force against the global consensus of the United Nations, which supports Namibia's independence and considers SWAPO the sole and authentic representative of the Namibian people. On the other hand, the global consensus in opposition to South African policies has expanded, and the study examines how the International Conference in Support of the Namibian People for Independence, held in Paris in 1983, revealed once again that the vast majority of the nations of the world are committed to the independence of Namibia. The study concludes with an examination of how the Non-

Aligned Movement has challenged the role of the Contact Group and its efforts to take the Namibian issue out of the auspices of the United Nations and to limit SWAPO's role in the settlement plan. It discusses why the Namibian issue should be returned to the United Nations and resolved through multilateral diplomacy. As a result, the United Nations has held a series of special meetings to discuss the Namibian situation, and the secretary-general has made a major effort to implement resolution 435. Finally, the study examines the recent effort of the Non-Aligned Movement at an extraordinary meeting of the Co-ordinating Bureau in New Delhi in April 1985 to give increased legitimacy to SWAPO. It concludes with an analysis of the movement's role at the June 1985 UN Security Council meeting on Namibia where it assisted in obtaining a consensus resolution calling for voluntary sanctions against South Africa. Thus the Non-Aligned Movement, which has played a historic role in internationalizing the question of Namibian independence, continues to play a significant part in supporting the rights of the Namibian people for self-determination and in pressuring the global community to fulfill its "sacred trust."

MAJOR EVENTS AND DECISIONS IN THE UNITED NATIONS
RELATING TO NAMIBIAN INDEPENDENCE

A Chronology

The following is a *brief* outline of some of the major events and decisions undertaken by the United Nations in its efforts to protect the rights of the Namibian people and in support of the independence of Namibia. These activities were largely a result of the demands of the Non-Aligned Movement, which was formed in 1961. (A more thorough discussion of United Nations activities can be found in the UN document *Namibia: A Unique UN Responsibility*.)

October 1961. UN General Assembly's Committee on South West
  Africa recommended the termination of South Africa's mandate
  to administer the territory and an immediate UN presence.
27 October 1966. The General Assembly (GA) reaffirmed the
  inalienable right of the people of South West Africa to self-
  determination, freedom and independence; terminated South
  Africa's mandate; and placed the territory under the direct
  responsibility of the UN. Resolution 2145.
19 May 1967. The GA created the UN Council for South West Africa
  to administer the territory with the active and full participation
  of its inhabitants until independence.
11 June 1968. The GA declared South West Africa to be known
  henceforth as Namibia in accordance with the wishes of its
  people; condemned the South African government for refusing
  to comply with UN resolutions and for its non co-operation with
  the Council for Namibia (formerly the Council for South West
  Africa); and condemned those states who continued to
  collaborate politically, economically, and militarily with South
  Africa thus contributing to its persistent defiance of the
  international community. Resolution 2372.
20 March 1969. The Security Council (SC) proclaimed South Africa in
  illegal occupation of Namibia and called for its immediate
  withdrawal from administration of the territory (with the U.K.
  and France abstaining). Resolution 264.
12 August 1969. The SC recognized the legitimate right of the people
  of Namibia to struggle against South African authorities illegally
  occupying their land and called for moral and material aid from
  all states to assist the Namibian people in their struggle. It also
  decided that South Africa's continued occupation of Namibia was
  an "aggressive encroachment" of UN authority, a violation of the
  territorial integrity, and a denial of the political sovereignty of
  the Namibian people and, therefore, called for South Africa to
  immediately withdraw from the territory. Resolution 269 was
  adopted with the U.K., France, the U.S., and Finland abstaining.
  Reaffirmed by the GA in December. Resolution 2517.
29 July 1970. The SC, with France and the U.K. abstaining, called
  upon all states to desist from any relations with South Africa and
  for states to curtail state and privately owned or operated
  enterprises with Namibia. Resolution 283.
9 December 1970. The GA condemned the economic assistance being
  given to South Africa by its allies. This included the corporate,
  trading, and financial interests that contribute to the exploitation
  of Namibia and its people.

21 June 1971. At the request of the SC for an advisory opinion, the International Court of Justice declared South Africa in illegal occupation of Namibia and obliged it to withdraw immediately.

20 October 1971. The SC agreed with the advisory opinion of the International Court of Justice and declared South Africa's refusal to withdraw as detrimental to peace and security in the region. Resolution 301.

4 February 1972. The SC asked the secretary-general to visit the region, meet with various parties concerned, and for the South African government to participate. In a report, 30 April 1973, the secretary-general concluded that the government of South Africa gave no indication that there was a serious intent on its part to proceed with the independence of Namibia in the very near future.

14 April 1973. The International Conference of Experts for the Support of the Victims of Colonialism and Apartheid in South Africa, held in Oslo, Norway, and organized by the UN and OAU, called for international support for the liberation struggle of the Namibian people and the recognition of SWAPO as their authentic representative.

14 June 1973. The Lusaka Declaration adopted by the UN Council for Namibia concluded that South Africa's continued illegal presence in Namibia seriously endangered global peace and security and called for the termination of the economic exploitation of Namibia by transnational corporations and of all support to South Africa whether it be political, economic, military, or financial.

12 December 1973. SWAPO is recognized by the GA as the sole and authentic representative of the Namibian people. Resolution 3111.

December 1974. The GA requested all member states to support and comply with the Decree for the Protection of Natural Resources of Namibia enacted by the UN Council for Namibia on 27 September 1974. This is known as Decree No. 1.

17 December 1974. The SC *unanimously* condemned South Africa's continued illegal occupation of Namibia and the maintenance of its apartheid system in the territory, including its bantustans policy and detention of political prisoners. The SC also demanded South Africa begin transferring power to the Namibian people through the auspices of the UN. Resolution 366.

30 January 1976. In its strongest and most comprehensive resolution to date, resolution 385, the SC *unanimously* condemned South

Africa for its continued illegal occupation of Namibia, its illegal apartheid practices in Namibia, its military build-up and use of the territory as a base to attack neighboring states, and its failure to comply with SC resolutions. Resolution 385 also declared that free elections under the supervision and control of the UN be held for the whole of Namibia as one political entity. It demanded South Africa accept the provisions for holding free elections giving adequate time and arrangements for the UN to establish the necessary machinery within Namibia to supervise and control such elections.

26 August 1976. The UN Institute for Namibia in Lusaka, Zambia was formally opened. It was established under a plan by the Council for Namibia to provide education, training, and research opportunities for Namibians in preparation for independence.

20 December 1976. The GA gave further recognition to SWAPO by supporting the armed struggle of the Namibian people for national independence and self-determination under SWAPO's leadership by inviting SWAPO to be an observer at GA sessions and designating that SWAPO be present at talks with South Africa for the transfer of power to the people of Namibia under UN auspices.

16–21 May 1977. UN Council for Namibia and the Special Committee of 24 on decolonization co-sponsored the International Conference in Support of the Peoples of Zimbabwe and Namibia in Maputo, Mozambique, which declared Walvis Bay an integral part of Namibia, rejecting South Africa's claim. The conference also denounced the Turnhalle tribal talks instigated by South Africa and reaffirmed UN responsibility for free elections for the whole of Namibia as one political entity.

4 November 1977. The GA recognized Walvis Bay as an integral part of Namibia and condemned South Africa's decision to annex the bay as illegal and an act of colonial expansion. It also called for a special session on Namibia in 1978.

4 November 1977. For the first time in UN history, the SC *unanimously* passed a resolution to impose a mandatory arms embargo against South Africa, including material that might be related to nuclear collaboration.

23 April–3 May 1978. The GA held a ninth special session specifically on the question of Namibia and adopted a Declaration and Programme of Action in support of its self-determination and independence.

6 May 1978. The SC condemned South Africa for invading Angola and using Namibia as a launching base. It also commended

Angola for its support of the people of Namibia in their struggle and demanded South Africa end its illegal occupation.

27 July 1978. The SC voted in favor of a proposed settlement on the question of Namibia's independence presented to it on April 25 by five Western members of the SC—Canada, France, the Federal Republic of Germany, the United Kingdom, and the United States. The proposal suggested among other recommendations that a special representative be appointed to ensure that free and fair elections based on an impartial electoral process be carried out in Namibia. The proposal had been previously accepted by South Africa on 25 April and by SWAPO on 12 July after some clarifications. Resolution 431.

29 August 1978. The secretary-general presented a report to the SC based on the findings of the UN commissioner for Namibia that the Western settlement proposal required the establishment of a United Nations Transition Assistance Group (UNTAG) in Namibia and would have to be implemented in stages.

29 September 1978. The SC approved the secretary-general's report on the implementation of the Contact Group's proposal for settling the Namibian question. It decided to establish UNTAG and welcomed SWAPO's efforts to co-operate and called upon South Africa to co-operate with the secretary-general in the implementation of the resolution. Resolution 435.

21 October 1978. The secretary-general indicated administrative arrangements for UNTAG were being established, but that the foreign ministers of the five Western governments, after meeting with South African officials in Pretoria, were unable to reconcile the decision of the government of South Africa to hold unilateral elections in December with the settlement proposal introduced by the Western governments, endorsed by the United Nations, and agreed to by South Africa.

13 November 1978. The SC condemned South Africa's decision to hold unilateral elections in Namibia from 4–8 December in defiance of the United Nations. Resolution 439.

21 December 1978. The GA also condemned South Africa's actions in defiance of SC resolutions and proclaimed 1979 the International Year of Solidarity with the People of Namibia.

31 May 1979. The GA determined that South Africa had "acted deceitfully through unilateral measures and sinister schemes" during discussions for a negotiated settlement of Namibia's independence.

2 November 1979. In reaction to South Africa's air and ground attacks against Angola on 28 October, the SC passed a resolution calling

upon South Africa to withdraw its armed forces from Angola
and demanding it desist from using Namibia to launch attacks
against Angola and other neighboring states.

7–11 July 1980. Twenty-four international experts gave testimony at
UN headquarters on the mining, transport, processing and sale
of Namibian uranium by South Africa and other foreign
economic interests in violation of Decree No. 1 at the UN
Council for Namibia's Hearings on the Plunder of Namibian
Uranium. Also exposed were the effects of uranium mining on
the health of Namibian miners and the environment.

11–13 September 1980. The International Conference in Solidarity with
the Struggle of the People of Namibia, initiated by SWAPO and
supported by the UN Council for Namibia, adopted a declaration
calling upon the international community to support the
legitimate struggle of the Namibian people.

19 January 1981. The secretary-general reported to the SC that,
unlike SWAPO, South Africa was not yet prepared to sign a
cease-fire to bring peace to Namibia nor to proceed with the
implementation of resolution 435. In the secretary-general's
opinion, South Africa's actions at the preimplementation meeting
in Geneva between SWAPO and South Africa "must give rise to
the most serious international concern."

2–6 March 1981. Highly critical of South Africa's actions at the
Geneva preimplementation meeting, the GA held the Pretoria
government responsible for the collapse of the meeting and
viewed South Africa's manner as obstructionist.

30 April 1981. Four SC draft resolutions that would have imposed
comprehensive and mandatory political, economic, and military
sanctions against South Africa, including an oil and arms
embargo are vetoed by three of its permanent members (France,
U.K., U.S.), but supported by a majority of SC members.

31 August 1981. The U.S. vetoed a SC draft resolution condemning
South Africa for its "premeditated unprovoked and persistent
armed invasion perpetrated against Angola and its utilization of
the illegally occupied territory of Namibia as a springboard for
armed invasions and destabilization of Angola."

3–14 September 1981. An eighth emergency special session of the GA
reaffirmed SC resolution 435 (1978) as the only basis for
peaceful settlement and firmly rejected the recent efforts of
certain members of the Contact Group to undermine the
international consensus for 435 and demanded its immediate
implementation.

10 December 1981. In a six-part resolution (36/121), the GA strongly

condemned South Africa for obstructing the implementation of
SC resolutions 385 (1976), 435 (1978), 439 (1978) and seriously
threatening international peace and security with its continued
illegal occupation of Namibia, its military aggression against
independent African states, its apartheid policies, and its
development of nuclear weapons. It strongly condemned the
collusion of such states as the United States, the Federal Republic
of Germany, and Israel in directly or indirectly facilitating South
Africa's nuclear capacity.

27 October 1982. The secretary-general expressed disappointment at
the delay in implementing SC resolution 435 during a Week of
Solidarity with the People of Namibia and Their Liberation
Movement.

20 December 1982. The GA reiterated its resolutions and firmly
rejected "the persistent attempts by the United States and South
Africa to establish any linkage or parallelism between the
independence of Namibia and any extraneous issue, in particular
the withdrawal of Cuban forces from Angola."

25–29 April 1983. The UN Council for Namibia sponsored the
International Conference in Support of the Struggle of the
Namibian People for the Independence in Paris. The vast
majority of countries rejected the introduction of extraneous
issues, such as the linkage concept, into the implementation of
resolution 435 and concluded that the negotiations for Namibia's
independence be returned to the United Nations.

19 May 1983. The secretary-general expressed his concern to the SC
for the delay in the implementation of resolution 435 and the
emergence of factors outside the scope of 435 which "hamper"
its implementation.

23 May–1 June 1983. The SC debated the question of Namibia.

20–28 October 1983. The SC debated the question of Namibia and
with the exception of the United States, which abstained, the
Contact Group countries rejected the linkage doctrine and
adopted resolution 539.

29 November–5 December 1983. The GA debated the question of
Namibia.

14 December 1983. In a letter to the president of the SC, Angola
lodged another complaint against South Africa after another
military attack and requested hearings on South Africa's war
against Angola.

15 December 1983. In a letter to the secretary-general, South Africa's
foreign minister indicated his government is "prepared to begin
a disengagement of forces which from time to time conduct

military operations against SWAPO in Angola, on 31 January 1984, on the understanding that this gesture would be reciprocated by the Angolan government."

19–20 December 1983. The SC debated the question of Namibia and South Africa's war against Angola.

29 December 1983. The secretary-general reported to the SC that South Africa had not responded in a definitive manner with regard to relevant decisions of the Security Council in the implementation of resolution 435 (1978).

1 January 1985. The SC approved resolution 546 condemning South Africa for its unprovoked attack on Angola. The United States and the U.K. abstained.

3 May 1985. The SC condemned and rejected South Africa's unilateral action to form an "interim government" in Namibia.

2: The Non-Aligned Movement and the Internationalization of the Namibian Question[1]

The illegal occupation of Namibia by the government of South Africa and the exploitation of the territory and its inhabitants have been the concern of many national, regional, and international groupings, both governmental and nongovernmental. Recently, the Reagan administration of the United States has taken an interest in Namibian independence and has claimed it has brought the matter close to a resolution. SWAPO President Sam Nujoma has stated to the contrary:

If the decolonization of Namibia is closer, it is mainly a result of intensification of the war by the military wing of SWAPO, which is inflicting heavy casualties on South African troops....

The Reagan administration should not credit itself with the efforts of the international community as a whole. Indeed, the credit for decolonizing Namibia would have to be accorded to the Namibian people, first and foremost, and to the OAU, the Non-Aligned Movement, and the UN and its specialized agencies, which have been assisting the Namibian people.[2]

Since the founding of the United Nations there has been a growing global consensus that the government of South Africa is a minority government and should not be recognized as a legitimate sovereign state until it changes its apartheid policy. Furthermore, there is a growing global consensus that the government of South Africa is in current and illegal control of Namibia. Many governments have indicated their unwillingness to accept the claim of the Republic of South Africa to be the protector of the Namibian people and to negotiate on their behalf. But in spite of the efforts of the global community, 1984 marked one hundred years of Namibian colonization.

No international grouping has played as significant a role in supporting the rights of the Namibian people and in promoting the independence of Namibia as the Non-Aligned Movement (NAM). Since its inception in 1961, the NAM has supported political independence and self-determination for all nations. As an international social movement of developing countries from Asia, Africa, Latin America and the Caribbean, the Arab world, and parts of Europe, it has defended decolonization and the right of self-determination globally, especially in the struggles in southern Africa. It has gained broad support for its principles, growing from its original 25 members to 102 at its most recent summit conference, its seventh, held in New Delhi in 1983. This movement has also established historical precedents in international relations by recognizing national liberation movements and provisional governments as legitimate representatives of states prior to complete and full independence. With the seating of the Provisional Government of Algeria at the first summit meeting of non-aligned countries in Belgrade in 1961 and later with the seating of Angola and Vietnam, the movement has accepted provisional governments as full members. National liberation movements are invited to attend non-aligned meetings and are given opportunities to address the members. SWAPO was at first a guest, then held observer status, from 1973, and became a full member of the movement in 1978. These actions have not only transformed the nature of international relations, but also influenced the workings of the United Nations. Through their activities and advocacy, non-aligned countries have played and continue to play a major role, especially at the United Nations, in keeping the issue of Namibian independence before the world community. They have also continuously pushed for the peaceful establishment of Namibia's independence under the auspices of the United Nations with SWAPO as the sole and authentic representative of the Namibian people. In their analysis of the Namibian issue and their support of specific resolutions at the United Nations, the non-aligned countries have even brought the Western European states to recognize the significance of Namibian independence. Most recently, they have exposed the liabilities of the Contact Group initiative in promoting Namibia's interests. They have thus marshaled support on the five continents for the inalienable rights of the Namibian people. In this way, the NAM has been crucial for internationalizing support for Namibia's independence.

Historically, the United Nations has viewed Namibia primarily as a mandate or trusteeship matter and consequently has treated it as a legal problem requiring·some form of juridical solution. Non-aligned countries, on the other hand, have always held a broader conception of the Namibian question. They have considered it a political issue, and specifically an issue of decolonization and independence. For the NAM, Namibia's independence is also an integral condition for the liberation of southern Africa and the entire African continent. More recently, non-aligned countries have begun to see it in its international context and have argued that the independence of Namibia and the right of self-determination of the Namibian people are critical to the maintenance of global peace and security.

The Namibian case dramatically involves all the principles of non-alignment—peace; independence; economic, social, and cultural equality; and the democratization of global decision-making—universal principles based on the United Nations Charter. Namibia represents the age-old question of independence and sovereignty. It concerns the matter of a just war of national liberation. It involves the right of Angola, an independent member of the movement, to seek support from another non-aligned country in order to defend itself from South African attacks. It reveals how transnational corporations have benefited from South Africa's continuous control of Namibia and how the governments of these corporations, namely, the United States, West Germany, France, Canada, and the United Kingdom have attempted to delay Namibian independence to guarantee transnational exploitation of Namibian uranium. It shows the pillage of the resources of southern Africa and how this could result in Namibia's becoming an economic calamity when it assumes state power. Namibia also raises another fundamental non-aligned concern—racism—and reveals how it remains a virulent force in world politics. It demonstrates how the Western media, the dominant information system in the world, has conveniently neglected to report the activities of SWAPO or to identify some of the villainous actions of the South African government. The plight and pain of the Namibian people is either omitted or distorted in the world's media, and thus even parts of Asia, Africa, and Latin America that are dependent on Western news sources for information remain ignorant of the struggle in Namibia. Finally, there is the question of Namibia's becoming a major conflict zone with the potential to spark a nuclear war. It shows how an independence movement can be perverted and transformed into an extension of the East-West conflict, turning all of southern Africa into a war zone. South Africa has developed nuclear capability and in its determination to defy the global community on matters of apartheid and Namibia, the Pretoria government could plunge the world into a nuclear holocaust. The Namibian question thus presents for non-aligned countries a dramatic illustration of why there is a need for them to exist as a movement and why they must continue to work for the achievement of Namibian independence.

Namibia has been an integral part of non-aligned history since the founding of the movement. At the first summit meeting in Belgrade, in 1961, twenty-five member states attended, along with three observer states and a number of other organizations, including national liberation movements. SWAPO was among the national liberation movements present, and Sam Nujoma, the president of SWAPO, was himself the representative. The non-aligned countries concluded at the Belgrade summit that colonialism, imperialism, neo-colonialism, and other forms of domination had to be eliminated. Only then could a lasting global peace be achieved. Toward this end, the non-aligned countries would encourage and support all peoples in their struggles for independence and equality.[3]

In 1964, the NAM held its second summit conference in Cairo.

Its membership had nearly doubled through the addition of many newly independent African countries. These African states helped to focus the movement's attention on the decolonization of the rest of the African continent. The heads of state issued a state-ment, "Concerted Action for the Liberation of·the Countries Still Dependent: Elimination of Colonialism, Neo-Colonialism and Imperialism."[4] They called for the full implementation of the United Nations declaration on the granting of independence to colonial countries and drew specific attention to the continuing struggles in Africa. On the question of Namibia, the movement reaffirmed "the inalienable right of the people of South West Africa to self-determination and independence" and condemned "the Government of South Africa for its persistent refusal to co-operate with the United Nations in the implementation of the pertinent resolutions of the General Assembly."[5]

In offering additional support for anticolonial struggles, the non-aligned countries condemned the use of force and other forms of intimidation and the intervention of colonial powers to prevent the exercise of the right of self-determination. They argued that colonized people might, if necessary, legitimately resort to the taking up of arms when their efforts to obtain self-determination and independence were persistently opposed. As early as 1964, the non-aligned countries recognized the right of a people to engage in armed struggle to achieve self-determination and independence, and thereafter, this stance was gradually accorded legitimacy within the international community at the United Nations.

For the NAM, the United Nations is the primary institution for global decision-making, for it provides a forum where small and middle-sized states can participate in international issues. It is to the United Nations that the non-aligned countries bring their declarations for action. The non-aligned countries faulted the West for enabling South Africa to continuously defy the United Nations. In 1966, led by the African states, the non-aligned countries made Namibia a major issue. Against the opposition of Western powers and the then pro-West Latin American countries, they sought an immediate end to South African rule in Namibia.

Through their efforts, the General Assembly in October 1966 approved resolution 2145, terminating South Africa's mandate and placing Namibia directly under the responsibility of the United Nations. In addition, the non-aligned built a coalition within the United Nations that resulted in the creation of the UN Council for South West Africa (later the UN Council for Namibia), which was to serve as the legal administrative authority of the territory until it obtained its independence. During the 1960s, the non-aligned countries also sought to get the Security Council, specifically its Western members, to take more decisive action with regard to the independence of Namibia, but they were less successful.[6] The reluctance of the West to bring pressure upon the South African government, as revealed by their abstentions from Security Council resolutions, angered and frustrated the movement. The abuse of power of the Security Council, notably the veto, was a common concern at non-aligned meetings.

Decolonization was the major political issue at the third summit of non-aligned countries, held in Lusaka, Zambia, in 1970. The upsurge of liberation struggles globally in the years since the Cairo summit was giving new hope to the African continent. Nearly all of Africa was free, except for the Portuguese colonies and southern Africa. The non-aligned countries passed a major thirteen-point resolution on Namibia as part of the Lusaka Manifesto for the decolonization of southern Africa. In detailed support of the independence of Namibia, they called for economic sanctions against South Africa, as outlined in the UN Charter, and demanded that governments, trade unions, and commercial firms refrain from relations with South Africa that would provide them with military assistance or weapons.[7]

In activities at the United Nations, the Non-Aligned Movement supported the efforts of the Council for Namibia to achieve a negotiated settlement for Namibia's independence. The Namibian people, on the other hand, faced with South African aggression and the refusal of the Pretoria government to negotiate, had taken to armed struggle under SWAPO's leadership several years before. By 1968, the Organization of African Unity had formally recognized SWAPO as the sole and authentic representative of the Namibian people. In 1972, the NAM also invited SWAPO to its foreign ministers' meeting in Georgetown, Guyana, with guest status. Since the colonial and racist governments continued to refuse to participate in the decolonization process in a peaceful manner, as exemplified by their rejection of the Lusaka Manifesto, the non-aligned countries agreed that there was an urgent need to assist legitimate armed struggle. At Georgetown, the foreign ministers considered ways and means to finance, arm, and train liberation movements in Africa.

The decade of the 1970s began brightly: there was some hope that the independence of Namibia was within reach. In June 1971, the International Court of Justice declared that South Africa was illegally occupying Namibia. That October, the Security Council agreed with the court's advisory opinion and concluded that South Africa's refusal to withdraw was a threat to regional peace and security. From September 1974 through November 1975, five former Portuguese colonies—Guinea-Bissau, Mozambique, Cape Verde, São Tome, and Angola—won their independence, largely through the formation of national liberation movements and armed struggle. The ongoing independence struggle in Zimbabwe was successfully completed in April 1980. These victories brought into power governments with radical nationalist and prosocialist tendencies and altered local, regional, and international politics. The response from South Africa and its Western Allies, as we shall discuss later in this study, was to view the changes in the region as a threat to their national security and as part of the East-West conflict. This response has served to delay the independence of Namibia.

The NAM, on the other hand, intensified its pursuit of Namibia's independence. The fourth summit conference, held in Algiers in 1973, was a watershed in the history of the NAM. Its declarations revealed the movement's increasingly radical orientation and militant stance. And attending the summit with observer status were fifteen national liberation movements or political parties, an unprecedented number, among them SWAPO.

The Algiers summit is primarily notable for producing an economic declaration that called for a New International Economic

Order (NIEO). However, the summit meeting also issued a separate Declaration on the Struggle for National Liberation. In it the non-aligned countries called for ways to "strengthen the military, economic, political, and moral support to liberation movements and to undertake all necessary measures to enable liberation movements to conclude their struggles successfully," as well as ways to mobilize public opinion in support of freedom and independence and to "isolate colonial, racist, and Apartheid regimes." In a specific resolution on Namibia, the movement joined with the OAU, the International Conference on Namibia (Brussels), and the Conference in Support of the Victims of Colonialism and Apartheid (Oslo), in recognizing SWAPO as the legitimate representative of the Namibian people.

The movement continued to support the efforts to achieve Namibia's independence under the auspices of the United Nations, fully aware that the Western powers were reluctant to increase international pressure on the government of South Africa. It was largely through the efforts of the non-aligned countries that SWAPO was recognized by the General Assembly in 1973 as the sole and authentic representative of the Namibian people. Resolution 3111 was not adopted unanimously, however, as South Africa and Portugal opposed this recognition, and seventeen states, largely from the West, abstained. Attempts in the Security Council to remove South Africa from the United Nations were also thwarted by the veto power of France, the United Kingdom, and the United States. However, the Security Council did unanimously support resolution 366 (1974). It condemned South Africa's continued illegal occupation of Namibia, called for the abolition of "it's racially discriminative and politically repressive laws and practices," and demanded Pretoria begin transferring power to the Namibian people through the auspices of the United Nations. With pressures mounting upon the Security Council to be more forceful, its members were giving a signal to South Africa that they expected the Pretoria government to make some demonstration of its good intentions.[8]

Non-aligned countries called for international support of SWAPO through the Council for Namibia to secure the inalienable rights of the Namibian people. They opposed the support certain Western powers were giving to the South African government and called attention to the presence in Namibia of a consulate of the Federal Republic of Germany, in violation of UN resolutions and the International Court of Justice opinions, and to the attempts by permanent members of the Security Council, especially the United Kingdom and France, to constrain the role of the UN Council for Namibia.

South Africa's response was to bypass the United Nations and SWAPO by setting up the so-called Windhoek "tribal talks," whereby the various ethnic or population groupings in Namibia were invited to participate in forming a constitution for eventual self-government. Neither SWAPO nor the NAM found this acceptable. They recognized that the South African government was attempting to control Namibia's future by placing in power those whom it favored or could control.

In the meetings that followed, the non-aligned countries continued to reaffirm the legitimate struggle of the Namibian people under the leadership of SWAPO and called for a resolution of the question of Namibia's independence under the auspices of the United Nations. At the Co-ordinating Bureau meeting in Havana, in March 1975, the movement supported the UN Council for Namibia Decree for the Protection of the Natural Resources of Namibia.[9] At the foreign ministers' conference in Lima that August, the non-aligned countries demanded that South Africa put into practice the resolutions and decisions of the United Nations and called for action from the Security Council.[10] At the Algiers Co-ordinating Bureau meeting in the summer of 1976, where the independence of Angola was welcomed, the non-aligned appealed to the international community to increase aid to liberation movements and expressed their concern over the continued support being given by "certain Western powers" to the racist South Africa government, which was carrying on a reign of terror throughout southern Africa. The movement also condemned the recent decision of the French government to provide nuclear reactors to South Africa as having a serious impact on peace and security in the region. Finally, the non-aligned recognized the important role that the front-line states were providing to the liberation struggles in the region and urged the international community to aid them.[11]

On January 30, 1976, as a result of the mounting efforts in support of Namibia's independence, the Security Council adopted resolution 385, its strongest and most comprehensive resolution to date. Its major innovation was its demand that South Africa hold elections for the whole of Namibia as one political entity under the supervision and control of the United Nations as soon as the United Nations could establish the necessary machinery.

In the meantime, Angola, Namibia's neighbor, had become a prominent feature of world news headlines. In the fall of 1975, the pro-West FNLA and UNITA, groupings backed by South Africa, militarily challenged the authority and leadership of the MPLA. To defeat the MPLA, South Africa, Zambia, and Zaire sent troops to Angola, and the United States lent aid and personnel through the Central Intelligence Agency. The victory of the MPLA—it was supported by invited Cuban troops—forced South Africa to withdraw its military forces from Angola in February 1976.[12] Resolution 385 and the Cuban troops issue were to be the focus of the international community in the years to come and they contributed to South Africa's digging in its heels on the question of Namibia's self-determination and independence.

The NAM had grown to 86 members when it held its fifth summit, in Colombo, Sri Lanka, in August 1976. Though the first summit to be held in Asia, it gave a great deal of attention to Africa's contribution to the movement. The movement recognized that Africa's firm anticolonial and antiracist commitments as well as the numerical strength of its states had been a major factor in the effectiveness of the non-aligned countries in promoting certain concerns at the United Nations. The heads of state concluded that:

The emancipation of Africa, the ending of racial discrimination against people of African origin all over the world, the protection of Africa from the rivalries of external powers, the de-nuclearization of Africa, and international co-operation for the economic and social development of Africa should not be merely regional or continental concerns but the priorities of the Non-Aligned Movement and of the United Nations.[13]

In support of Namibia, the movement established a Solidarity Fund for the liberation of southern Africa. It also condemned the South African government for its continued illegal occupation of Namibia, its militarization of the territory in order to repress the indigenous Namibian people, and its use of Namibia as a base for military attacks against neighboring states. Non-aligned countries commended Cuba and other states for assisting the people of Angola against the expansionist and colonialist activities of South Africa and its allies. They denounced South Africa's unilateral attempt to establish a settlement through the so-called Windhoek constitutional talks as an effort to retain control of Namibia and opposed the continued support being given by some Western powers to South Africa. The movement urged the international community not to recognize any puppet regime installed by South Africa in Namibia and called upon the Security Council to live up to its resolution 385, of January 30, 1976, on the holding of free elections in Namibia under the supervision and control of the United Nations. Once again the movement reiterated that any meaningful talks for the transference of power had to include SWAPO, the genuine representative of the Namibian people, under the auspices of the United Nations.[14]

At the Co-ordinating Bureau meeting in New Delhi in April 1977 non-aligned foreign ministers were faced with the problem of South Africa's increased aggression. The movement called for more assistance to the liberation movements in southern Africa, including contributions to the Non-Aligned Support and Solidarity Fund. Being fully aware of the importance of mobilizing international public opinion, the Bureau urged support for the forthcoming International Conference in Support of the People of Zimbabwe and Namibia in Maputo, Mozambique, in May 1977, and the World Conference for Action Against Apartheid in Lagos, in August 1977.

The Bureau meeting in Havana in May 1978 welcomed the holding of a special session on Namibia by the UN General Assembly, one which the movement had played a major role in calling. The non-aligned countries commended all governments for adopting the UN Declaration and Programme of Action on Namibia. The Bureau, however, concluded that the situation in southern Africa was worsening and that South Africa had no intention of withdrawing peacefully from Namibia. The movement therefore condemned South Africa for its nuclear buildup, its militarization of Namibia, its acts of aggression against neighboring independent African states, especially its use of Namibia once again on May 4, 1978, to invade Angola, and its apartheid and bantustanization policies in Namibia, which were intended to divide the people and foster civil war. The non-aligned countries rejected South Africa's attempts to find an "internal settlement" to the question of Namibia's independence through the sponsorship of the Turnhalle Constitutional Conference. They were also vehemently opposed to South Africa's promotion of the belief that the struggle of the Namibian people for self-determination was externally motivated. South Africa's designs on Namibia had become all too evident during its recent attempt to annex Walvis Bay. Thus the movement called for maximum pressure to be brought against South Africa to compel it to leave Namibia.[15]

The United Nations Council for Namibia attended the foreign ministers' meeting of non-aligned countries in Belgrade in July 25–30, 1978 with guest status. In assessing the current international situation, the movement identified as the primary feature "the struggle for the full political and economic emancipation of peoples and countries which are resolutely striving for free development and against all forms of exploitation and dependence. No people will reconcile itself to foreign interference and the imposition of alien will."[16] Non-aligned countries cited the ongoing national liberation struggles, particularly in Zimbabwe, Namibia, Palestine, South Africa, and other dependent and occupied territories, as demonstrations of resoluteness, determination, and sacrifice for freedom. They emphasized once again that South Africa's illegal occupation of Namibia was not only an aggression against the people of Namibia but also a challenge to the United Nations, which is responsible for the territory. In anticipation of the Security Council's consideration of the question of Namibia, the movement sent a cable to the president of the Security Council in support of the inalienable rights of the Namibian people and of SWAPO as the legitimate representative of the Namibian people. The NAM also restated its position that negotiations for independence were to be conducted with SWAPO under the auspices of the United Nations.[17]

The Security Council met the same week as the Belgrade meeting to consider a settlement proposal presented to it by a group of five of its Western members—Canada, France, the Federal Republic of Germany, the United Kingdom, and the United States. Among the recommendations of this Contact Group initiative, as it came to be known, was that a special representative be appointed to ensure that free and fair elections would be carried out in Namibia on the basis of an impartial electoral process. This recommendation was adopted by the Security Council on July 27, 1978, as resolution 431, which became the basis for resolution 435, adopted September 29, 1978, upon which negotiations for Namibia's independence under the auspices of the United Nations now rest. Resolution 435 approved the secretary-general's report, based on the findings of a special representative, and established the United Nations Transition Assistance Group (UNTAG) under the authority of the Security Council for the implementation of free and fair elections under the supervision and control of the United Nations. Resolution 435 also noted SWAPO's willingness to co-operate and its readiness to sign and observe a cease-fire and called upon South Africa to co-operate immediately with the implementation of the secretary-general's report.

Encouraged by these developments, non-aligned countries increased their support for SWAPO at an extraordinary meeting in New York at the United Nations on October 2, 1978. They considered the establishment of UNTAG a critical stage in the liberation struggle of Namibia and made SWAPO a full member of the NAM.[18]

The Maputo Extraordinary Meeting on Southern Africa

The severity and urgency of the situation in southern Africa led non-aligned countries to call an extraordinary ministerial meeting of the Co-ordinating Bureau in Maputo, Mozambique, January 26 through February 2, 1979. After initially agreeing to resolution 435, South Africa militarily invaded Angola to strike a blow at SWAPO and introduced unilateral elections for Namibia under its own auspices. The Maputo meeting was the first non-aligned gathering to concentrate on the problems of a single region. It was called exclusively "to consider the situation in southern Africa and to reiterate the collective solidarity and unflinching support of the non-aligned countries to the peoples of southern Africa at this critical and decisive phase in their struggle for freedom from colonialism, racism, racial discrimination and Apartheid and the attainment of their unalienable right to self-determination and national independence."[19]

The decision to hold the extraordinary meeting in Mozambique, one of the front-line states, and a country whose people had successfully waged a national liberation struggle against Portuguese colonialism, was itself a statement of confidence. At the opening session, President Samora Machel of Mozambique pointed out the meaning of the gathering. One of the primary goals of the NAM has been to emancipate subjugated people from racial, colonial, and imperialist domination and exploitation. He stated that the movement had achieved many successes because members agreed on a number of basic principles. Southern Africa, however, remained a region in which the fundamental principles of non-alignment were being contested and denied to the peoples of Namibia, Zimbabwe, and South Africa. This was a unique opportunity to demonstrate the measures being taken internationally to provide support for national liberation movements in southern Africa and the front-line states in their struggle against apartheid and the repressive South African government.[20]

The Maputo meeting was extremely intense. There was high praise for the victory of the African peoples over Portuguese colonialism and for the recent military victory of Angola over the invading army of South Africa. These victories gave new courage to national liberation struggles in southern Africa. There was also great commendation for the efforts of the peoples of southern Africa to achieve their freedom and self-determination through peaceful means, especially their attempts to negotiate a peaceful transition to independence. The Co-ordinating Bureau severely criticized the minority regimes in southern Africa for their continued efforts to maintain political and military control of the region and for their exploitation of the indigenous people and natural resources.

Non-aligned countries observed that the successes of national liberation in Africa had dealt a serious blow to imperialism, but that South Africa's response had been to intensify internal suppression and invade neighboring states to eliminate national liberation movements and maintain its dominance in the region. Thus there was also severe criticism of the persistent support being given by some Western countries to the illegal, racist, minority regimes of southern Africa, whether it was in the form of financial investment, technology, or military and political aid. For this support only served to strengthen the will and capability of these regimes to threaten international peace and security.[21]

The Maputo resolution on Namibia included support for the liberation struggle and a request for additional support for SWAPO in its political and diplomatic efforts as well as its armed struggle to achieve independence. The Bureau opposed the attempts by South Africa to dismember Namibia by annexing Walvis Bay and by establishing a puppet government. The non-aligned countries condemned the so-called elections arranged by South Africa of December 4, 1978, and the association of certain Western governments with these elections as an endangerment of the international effort under the auspices of the United Nations to achieve a genuine and peaceful settlement of the issue of Namibia. They called for vigilance against further attempts to delay Namibia's independence. Finally, they reiterated their support for the UN effort, especially Security Council resolution 435 (1978) and other UN resolutions, and rejected any settlement that did not include SWAPO. In further support of SWAPO, the Bureau decided to establish a Special Non-Aligned Fund for SWAPO.[22]

In Colombo, June 4–9, 1979, the Co-ordinating Bureau reaffirmed the Maputo Communiqué and expressed its disappointment with the slow rate of political change in southern Africa.

The movement reiterated its position on the legitimate right to armed struggle. The non-aligned countries recognized that national liberation movements had no option but to take to armed struggle to obtain freedom when regimes "with the tacit connivance of their imperialist supporters" resolutely refuse to consider a peaceful transition to independence and persistently renege on previously agreed to and arranged negotiations "with apparent impunity." The Bureau, therefore, gave its full support to the legitimate armed struggle of the peoples of Namibia, Zimbabwe, and South Africa and cited the United States, France, the United Kingdom, Israel, Japan, Belgium, and Italy as major collaborators with the Pretoria government in its racist and imperialist policies in southern Africa.[23]

The sixth summit conference of heads of state or government of non-aligned countries met in Havana, Cuba, in September, 1979, and once again strongly condemned South Africa for its "stubborn refusal" to withdraw from Namibia and for its delaying tactics carried on with the "complicity and encouragement of Imperialist Powers." It deplored the efforts of imperialists to isolate and destroy national liberation movements. It condemned the formation of new military alliances, such as those linking South Africa and Israel, that perpetuated racism and encouraged conflict and instability in the region.[24] It specifically denounced South Africa's attempts to arrange an "internal solution" by imposing an arbitrary "National Assembly" and puppet government in Namibia. The non-aligned countries resolutely declared that they would neither recognize nor work with any so-called "National Assembly" or puppet government, as they were illegal and in contradiction with the resolutions of the United Nations, the Organization of African Unity, and the Non-Aligned Movement.[25]

Non-aligned foreign ministers next met in New Delhi, India, February 9–13, 1981, a month after the failed Geneva meeting between South Africa and SWAPO had been convened by the United Nations to implement the UN plan. The purpose of this preimplementation meeting was to establish a date for a ceasefire and the placement of UNTAG in accordance with Security Council resolution 435 (1978). The non-aligned charged South

Africa with duplicity and arrogance for deliberately sabotaging the Geneva meeting. They noted the "apparent reluctance" of the Contact Group to "use their enormous influence and leverage on South Africa" and expressed their regret that the group had not played a more constructive role in ensuring that South Africa cooperate with the secretary-general in implementing the UN plan. They also condemned the continued economic, military, and nuclear aid being given to South Africa by a number of Western countries, as in their view such aid only served to sustain apartheid.

The movement reaffirmed its support of SWAPO as the sole and authentic representative of the Namibian people and commended its statesmanship. It gave its continued support to the UN Council for Namibia as the only legal administering authority over the territory until independence. Given that South Africa was responsible for the failure of the Geneva meeting, the foreign ministers called on the UN Security Council to "impose comprehensive mandatory economic sanctions under Chapter VII of the United Nations Charter to compel the Pretoria regime to terminate its illegal occupation of Namibia." If this should fail, they recommended the calling of an emergency special session of the UN General Assembly at the foreign ministers level for the specific purpose of reviewing the question of Namibia and to take appropriate measures as outlined by the UN Charter. It was clear to the NAM that the Contact Group initiative was inoperative and indeed was becoming an obstruction to the UN effort to achieve Namibia's independence. They concluded that increased pressure on South Africa was needed. As an additional step towards mobilizing world opinion and to demonstrate international support for the Namibian people in their legitimate struggle for self-determination and independence, the non-aligned countries decided to hold an extraordinary meeting of the movement specifically on the question of Namibia.[26]

The Algiers Extraordinary Meeting on Namibia

The future of southern Africa was in a critical position in the spring of 1981. In the United States, the new Reagan administration had given notice that it intended to alter America's policy toward South Africa by strengthening relations with Pretoria. Moreover, the Reagan administration reopened the Cold War and viewed any social and political change globally within the context of East-West relations. On the eve of the extraordinary non-aligned meeting, the front-line states held a summit meeting in Luanda, April 15, and reviewed the threats and direct attacks against their sovereignty and security with specific attention to the attempts to destabilize Angola. The Luanda summit condemned the new American efforts to legitimize the South African government and called for the implementation of Security Council resolution 435 "without any further delay, prevarication, qualification or modification." It also called for the Contact Group to assume its responsibility and exert the required pressure on South Africa to comply with the UN plan.[27]

The non-aligned countries held an extraordinary ministerial meeting of the Co-ordinating Bureau on the question of Namibia in Algiers, April 16–18, 1981. Its purpose was "to evaluate the situation in Namibia and to take specific measures for strengthening all forms of aid in support of the struggle of the Namibian people under the direction of SWAPO, its sole and authentic representative." The fact that a special meeting was called on a single issue indicated the high priority that non-aligned countries gave to Namibia's independence. The meeting had been initiated by Algeria, which had waged a bitter armed struggle against a colonial power to win independence, and had remained in the forefront of the struggles to liberate the African continent. Just prior to the meeting, Algerian President Chadli Benjedid made a tour of the major states in Africa to re-emphasize the support of independent countries for those still under colonial, imperialist, and racist domination.

The meeting was a major demonstration of non-aligned support for SWAPO and for UN efforts to achieve a peaceful solution to Namibia's continued illegal occupation and exploitation by South Africa and its allies. It condemned South Africa's policies in Namibia and its systematic "policy of destabilization, provocation, and aggression" in the region. Most important, the non-aligned countries severely condemned the role of the Contact Group and its relationship with South Africa. While the failure of the Geneva preimplementation meeting was just another indication of South Africa's determination to maintain control of Namibia, it also revealed that the Contact Group lacked the will to exert pressure on the South African government to comply with resolution 435 and the plan of negotiated settlement which they themselves had voluntarily initiated.

The efforts of the Contact Group, the non-aligned argued, had served to delay Namibia's independence and to take the negotiations process outside the auspices of the United Nations. While the global community had sought to isolate the South African government for its policies, the efforts of the Contact Group had served to bolster South Africa and give legitimacy to Pretoria's racist and militaristic policies in southern Africa. In addition, the foreign ministers condemned the actions of certain Western governments, especially the United States, for turning the question of Namibia's independence into a regional security problem tied to the East-West conflict. Thus the efforts of the United States to destabilize Angola in pursuit of its own interests, including the proposed repeal of the Clark amendment, in order to contain what it views as the expanding influence of the East at the expense of the West, had served to encourage South Africa's policy of aggression against SWAPO and the front-line states. SWAPO spoke out specifically against the use of ideological warfare as another weapon to attack national liberation movements. As an example, it was pointed out that the West introduced code words such as "international terrorism" to delegitimize the just struggle of peoples for self-determination.[28] Moreover, the Bureau was highly critical of the contributions that Western powers had made to South Africa's military capabilities, notably its nuclear development, and expressed grave concern at reports that a military alliance was being created in the South Atlantic region to link certain Western countries with South Africa and other states. Consequently, they concluded that the global community's desire for a peaceful transition to independence for Namibia, under the auspices of the United Nations in accordance with its Charter, was being turned into a regional problem tied to the East-West conflict potentially threatening international peace and security.

The non-aligned countries asserted that the continued and illegal occupation of Namibia, the repression of its people, and the exploitation of its resources was a universal matter. They deplored the shift in concern from human and political rights to national interests, whether they were political, strategic, or economic. The movement demanded the implementation of UN Security Council resolution 435 and gave its full support to SWAPO and all the UN resolutions. Thus the *volte-face* of certain Western governments was exposed and condemned along with the collaboration of the Contact Group with South Africa and their delaying tactics. The non-aligned concluded that the United Nations needed to assume greater control of the negotiations process and passed a plan of action that included appealing to the Security Council to impose global mandatory sanctions against South Africa and encouraging all member states to participate in the forthcoming Security Council session on Namibia.[29]

From Algiers, the non-aligned representatives returned to the United Nations to urge the Security Council to take firm action against South Africa. The movement had hoped that the Security Council would impel and promote the just cause of the Namibian people. At their foreign ministers meeting at the United Nations in September 1981, they deplored the April 30 action of three Western permanent members of the Security Council, France, the United Kingdom, and the United States, in their veto of resolutions proposing comprehensive and mandatory sanctions against South Africa under Chapter VII of the UN Charter. In their opinion, the Security Council had "fallen short of its fundamental responsibility for the maintenance of international peace and security."[30]

The following year, on October 4–9, 1982, the non-aligned foreign ministers came together again to condemn South Africa's continued aggression against the front-line states, reject the linkage doctrine that had been added to the negotiations process, and reassert the legitimacy of the United Nations in resolving the question of Namibian independence.[31]

The seventh summit of non-aligned countries, the largest gathering to date of this international movement, met in New Delhi, India, on March 7–11, 1983. At this conference over one hundred members, along with more than a dozen observer countries, organizations, and national liberation movements, as well as many more guest delegations, reaffirmed earlier non-aligned resolutions with regard to Namibia.

In observing recent events to obtain the implementation of the UN plan for the independence of Namibia, the non-aligned countries were highly critical of the delays. They noted South Africa's "intransigence and persistent refusal" to comply with the various resolutions. They called attention to South Africa's persistent attempts to maintain colonial domination of Namibia, most recently through fraudulent constitutional and political schemes. They denounced these activities and urged all states not to recognize any entity formed through an "internal" settlement.

The non-aligned countries strongly condemned the U.S. policy of "constructive engagement" with the South African government. This new policy was not only undermining the international campaign to isolate South Africa for its apartheid system, but was giving Pretoria the courage to intensify its internal repression, escalate military assaults against neighboring states, and openly defy the world community on the question of Namibia's independence. They spelled out their views on the linkage issue in the following resolution:

The Heads of State or Government expressed their deep concern that Namibia's independence continued to be obstructed by the intransigence and persistent refusal of the racist regime of South Africa to comply with the relevant United Nations resolutions and decisions on Namibia, in particular, resolution 435 (1978). They reiterated the strong view of the non-aligned countries that the United Nations Security Council resolution 435 (1978) remained the only basis for the peaceful settlement of the Namibian question. In this connection, the Conference most categorically rejected the linkage or parallelism being drawn by the United States Administration between the independence of Namibia and the withdrawal of Cuban forces from Angola. This continued insistence constitutes an unwarranted interference in the internal affairs of the People's Republic of Angola.

The Heads of State or Government called upon the United Nations Security Council to meet, as soon as possible, in order to consider further action on the implementation of its Plan for Namibia's independence thereby assuming its primary responsibility for implementation of Security Council resolution 435 (1978).[32]

The non-aligned countries considered the linkage doctrine introduced by the United States to be "extraneous," "incompatible with the letter and spirit of Security Council resolution 435," and "an unwarranted interference in the internal affairs" of Angola. In short, the summit opposed the linkage doctrine as another "impediment" to the implementation of the UN plan for the independence of Namibia and was alarmed that the Contact Group seemed unable to detach or disassociate itself from this principally American concern.

The late Prime Minister of India, Mrs. Indira Gandhi, who chaired the meeting, spoke for the movement when she stated: "The other notorious outlaw is the South African regime, which defies the international family with impunity. It has been rightly observed that the very existence of the Government of Pretoria, which institutionalizes racism, negates the oneness of the human race. Aggression against its own people, and those of Namibia and other neighbors, is an affront."[33]

The movement thus revealed how the legitimate struggle of the Namibian people has been manipulated by South Africa and its allies. Even the most conservative and pro-American countries of the NAM were unable to associate themselves with the policies of the United States and other members of the Contact Group. For while a number of countries submitted reservations on some questions, such as those involving Puerto Rico and Palestine, they were unanimously agreed on the matters of southern Africa and Namibia.

The non-aligned countries reaffirmed their support for Namibia in New Delhi and designated thirty-one of their foreign ministers to follow up their resolution at the United Nations. However, in spite of these concerted efforts the government of South Africa and its supporters continue to defy the international community and delay Namibia's independence. The non-aligned countries recognized the power of this new conservative coalition and informed the president of SWAPO, Sam Nujoma, at the New Delhi summit that they were committed to supporting the Namibian people in their just cause, with arms, if necessary.[34] The NAM had long ago arrived at a consensus on the Namibian question. They now prepared for an international conference in Paris at which they hoped to expand and reaffirm the global solidarity for the struggles of the people of Namibia to attain their independence.

3: The Contact Group and the New Cold War Doctrine

To completely comprehend the postponement of Namibian independence requires an understanding of the grand design of the Republic of South Africa. Acting in concert with the nations of the Contact Group, South Africa has continuously ignored world opinion of its apartheid system and the illegal colonization of Namibia and defied the efforts of the global community to isolate it. It has had a consistent and well-developed regional strategy linking economic, political, diplomatic, and military objectives. The plan began with the idea of developing the front-line states into a *cordon sanitaire* of weak states on South Africa's northern border. The emergence of liberation movements there, however, and the success of Angola, Mozambique, and Zimbabwe in obtaining independence, led to a modification of this policy. South Africa then put into motion its military strategy—quick strikes into neighboring states—to delegitimize and destabilize individual governments. It also devised a strategy of creating within the front-line states dissident groups that would make secessionist demands. This involves leashing and unleashing individuals and groups, such as Savimbi and UNITA. Added to this was South Africa's capability of manipulating the economic well-being of the region. In the diplomatic arena, South Africa has skillfully managed contradictions in world politics to its benefit, especially East-West tensions, and has most recently used a number of governments, notably the Contact Group, to thwart the efforts of the global consensus on securing Namibia's independence. In the past decade, the South African government has made major gains by bypassing the global consensus, developed in the 1960s, that sought to isolate it because of its apartheid and colonialist policies. The intervention of the Contact Group in the negotiations for the independence of Namibia and South Africa's use of the Contact Group's role removed the Namibian question from a global multilateral forum to a regional big-power forum and also lent credibility to the South African government. Consequently, South Africa's most remarkable achievement has been the displacement of the negotiations for Namibian independence from the auspices of the United Nations and the acquisition of increased legitimacy for its government which has hitherto been treated as a pariah state by the international community for its apartheid policies.

In the beginning, the Contact Group, comprised of five Western members of the Security Council—Canada, France, the Federal Republic of Germany, the United Kingdom, and the United States—handled the Namibian question within the UN system. These nations had assumed, because of their special relationship with South Africa, that they were capable of influencing South Africa's policy toward Namibia. South Africa, in turn, assumed that in working through the Contact Group its proposals for Namibia might be found acceptable by the United Nations and it could claim to be a responsible member of the global community.

The framework for the Contact Group and resolution 435 was originally developed by the United States under the Carter administration. Highly supportive of a solution to the Namibian issue because of its human rights policies, attention to developing countries, and the appointment of Andrew Young as Ambassador to the United Nations and Donald McHenry as the deputy, the Carter administration initiated the formation of the Contact Group as a mediating force to facilitate negotiations between the South African government and the United Nations. Though skeptical of this arrangement, African states were persuaded through the presence and diplomacy of Andrew Young to give the Contact Group an opportunity to achieve its objective.[35]

In April 1978, the Contact Group presented the Security Council with a new proposal for settling the Namibian question, resolution 435. The flurry of activity on the part of the Contact Group around resolution 435 and its supposed leverage with the South African government suggested to the global community that a solution was imminent. South Africa's response, however, was to increase its aggression against neighboring states and SWAPO and to remain intransigent throughout the negotiations process.

The Reagan administration subsequently accepted and expanded the framework of the Contact Group, but altered the U.S. position towards the government of South Africa. The advent of the Reagan administration and its efforts to create a global conservative coalition, principally with Prime Minister Thatcher of the United Kingdom, brought a new dimension to the Namibian issue by consciously seeking to improve South Africa's status as an outcast nation and involve the South African government in "constructive engagement," not only with the United States and the West, but with the global community. South Africa is viewed as strategically, militarily, politically, and economically essential to Western interests. As South Africa is militarily the most powerful and aggressive country in the region, the United States and other Western powers have given South Africa the increased responsibility of maintaining regional security. The importance of that task therefore necessitates a closer relationship with the West as a counter to the forces of change in the region, which are viewed by the United States as a challenge to Western concerns.

This new relationship of "constructive engagement" between the United States and the South Africa was a consequence of the reopening of the Cold War in the late 1970s. American administrations increasingly viewed social change in the third world through the lens of the East-West conflict rather than recognizing the authenticity of anticolonial and anti-imperialist struggles. Long before the introduction of the issue of Cuban troops into the Namibian negotiations, the linkage doctrine, developed by former Secretary of State Henry Kissinger, later implemented by National Security Advisor Zbigniew Brzezinksi, and perfected by Ambassador Jeane Kirkpatrick, identified all regional conflicts within a framework of East-West global confrontations. In their view, movements for social and political change, including independence and social justice, do not have an indigenous basis, but are the result of external influences, i.e., the Soviet Union or its surrogates. Therefore, these movements are a threat to the security of the United States, the Western world, and its allies in the third world. Implicit in this doctrine is the racist assumption that peoples of color are incapable of determining their own destiny. Furthermore, these Western powers have redefined the nature of national liberation movements by characterizing them as illegitimate international "terrorist" organizations. In their view, national liberation movements are to be quickly and precisely eliminated before they become major movements for social and political change. Movements with broad national and international support are subject to a variety of efforts to destabilize and delegitimize them. By this definition, SWAPO is unacceptable as the sole and authentic representative of the Namibian people.

For the region, the consequences of this framework of global politics have been twofold. Firstly, the legitimacy of the South African government, which had previously been globally isolated, has been enhanced. Secondly, the resolution of the Namibian question has not been facilitated, as originally planned, but seriously complicated. The most articulate spokesperson for this new framework is U.S. Assistant Secretary of State, Chester Crocker:

U.S. officials correctly insist that the timetable and the blueprint for change in South Africa are not for outsiders to impose. Yet, without Western engagement in the region as a whole, it will not be possible to assure that South Africans are permitted to build their own future....

The real choice we will face in southern Africa in the 1980s concerns our readiness to compete with our global adversary in the politics of a changing region whose future depends on those who participate in shaping it. The choice has global implications, but the immediate decisions are, more often than not, regional ones....

Constructive engagement in the region as a whole is the only basis for Western credibility in Salisbury and Maputo. Our credibility in Moscow and Havana depends on adopting a strong line against the principle of introducing external combat forces into the region - a message best communicated by greater reliability in U.S. performance worldwide. There can be no presumed communist right to exploit and militarize regional tensions, particularly in this region where important Western economic, resource and strategic interests are exposed.

Another useful building block is the widely accepted understanding that European-American collaboration and mutual respect are the only valid base for any future undertakings directed toward South Africa— on Namibia or other issues. Similarly, we should continue the readiness under recent U.S. administrations to bring our policies out into the open and to meet publicly with South Africa's top leadership when circumstances warrant it.[36]

Mr. Crocker has also indicated some conditions for settling Namibia's independence under the UN plan.

A Namibia settlement is, we believe, desirable and obtainable at an early date. To succeed, it must be internationally acceptable—under UN auspices and in accordance with UNSC RES 435, which must form the basis of a settlement. That framework in our view, can and should be supplemented by additional measures aimed at reassuring all Namibian parties of fair treatment and at answering certain basic constitutional questions prior to elections that will lead to independence. A Namibia settlement, to be successful, must offer a genuine and equitable resolution of the conflict and lead the way toward an independence that strengthens, not undermines, the security of Southern Africa.

Clearly the relationship between Namibia and Angola cuts both ways. . . . I would like to emphasize that we are not laying down preconditions to any party. . . . We believe that movement on Namibia can reinforce movement toward Cuban withdrawal—and vice versa. Furthermore, we are convinced that a satisfactory outcome can only be based on parallel movement in both areas.[37]

South Africa had no difficulty in accepting this new American framework, since it needed support in confronting the regional consensus of the front-line states, the continental consensus of Africa, and the international consensus of the NAM. By linking the strategic, economic, and political interests of the Contact Group with its own national concerns, South Africa was able to develop new strategies for the postponement of Namibian independence. The new South African strategy was designed not only to destroy the global consensus in support of Namibia's independence and SWAPO, but to provide legitimacy for itself through its Western allies and to discredit the United Nations and its authority. The strategy that emerged after 1978 can be subcategorized as follows:

- Divide the front-line states by engaging in a policy of bilateral negotiations.
- Divide the OAU by cultivating allies on the continent who have some objection to the participation of non-African troops in the region.
- Divide the Non-Aligned Movement again by cultivating factions within the movement, especially with those countries in Asia and Latin America that are not directly linked with the African crisis.
- Prevent Western countries, such as the United Kingdom, France, and West Germany, from pursuing policies that would jeopardize Western security and economic interests in Africa.
- Destroy the legitimacy and effectiveness of the United Nations system by removing the Namibian question from the auspices of the United Nations and by eliminating a major role for SWAPO in an independent Namibia.

Thus a solution was devised that, in the final analysis, excludes the United Nations.

While South Africa effectively manipulated and developed its strategy, the Contact Group's interests gradually coincided more and more with South Africa's interests, making it difficult for an observer to distinguish, at any given moment, between the policies and objectives of South Africa and those of the Contact Group. Such a conceived structure has results in South Africa and the Contact Group constantly raising three specific issues in the negotiations. They are:

- The removal of South Africa's status as an outcast state in the international community.
- The determination of the particular character of the electoral system to be adopted in Namibia and how it is to be administered in order to ensure the exclusion of SWAPO as the sole and authentic representative of the Namibian people.
- The removal of Cuban forces from Angola as a precondition to an election (in Namibia).

Since 1978, South Africa has carefully cultivated the view that once Namibian independence was granted under SWAPO, the Western alliance would face a string of hostile nations in southern

Africa. South Africa has no intention of accepting a solution for Namibia that includes SWAPO except, at best, as a member of a coalition government with minority status. Thus, some members of the Contact Group have come to accept the South African thesis that an internationally acceptable formula should not involve SWAPO as the sole and authentic representative of the Namibian people as agreed to by the people of Namibia and the global community.

The strategy developed by the Republic of South Africa and the Contact Group for dealing with the Namibian question was actually two-pronged, with internal and external components. The internal aspect was meant to weaken SWAPO both militarily and electorally. Electoral tactics were devised to ensure that SWAPO could not form a government even if duly elected. South Africa argued along with the Contact Group that SWAPO must constantly make concessions at the constitutional level if the stalemate over the discussion was to be broken. But as discussions progressed, it became clear that these constitutional options were introduced on a number of occasions to delay the proceedings and involve the entire UN system, effectively steering the negotiations into a quagmire. Thus much time and effort were wasted in debates on the details of the various electoral systems to be adopted. The underlying assumption was that these delaying tactics could only result in the strengthening of other groups within Namibia. Consequently, South Africa used the delay to create a new coalition in Namibia, the infamous Turnhalle Alliance. Yet, the very necessity of these electoral manipulations proved once again that SWAPO retained its support among the people of Namibia and that South Africa was not ready to negotiate Namibia's independence as long as SWAPO had a popular majority.

South Africa's military strategy internally within the region has been to separate Namibian and Angolan interests. Namibia is to serve as a weak buffer state between Angola and South Africa. Internal conflicts within Angola are to be exploited, largely through the encouragement of secessionist groups, which keep the government from developing a strong national policy and threatens to partition the state. This divisiveness is supported by South Africa with the hopes that new political entities more favorable to South African interests will emerge. Hence the plan developed for Angola is a model to be applied to other frontline states, one that would eventually result in the bantustanization of southern Africa.

The external aspect of the South Africa-Contact Group strategy can be summed up in the "linkage" doctrine. The linkage doctrine, a new interpretation of U.S. and Western national interests, brings a number of external components, especially the concept of regional security and the East-West conflict, to the settlement of Namibia's independence. The regional security doctrine forges links between the national interests of the Contact Group states and especially those of the United States, with South African interests to oppose changing social and political forces in the region. It includes establishing South Africa as the dominant power in the region and legitimizing its status as an acceptable member of the global community. The security of the Republic of South Africa becomes dependent upon manipulating the internal politics of the front-line states to suit the needs of the Pretoria government. In conjunction with linking the Namibian question to the internal politics of Angola, South Africa seeks to give legitimacy to secessionist movements in Angola, such as UNITA, which it has sponsored. Thus the question of Namibian independence is also entangled in the security of the apartheid regime of South Africa in the region. The Contact Group initiative, therefore, must be seen within the larger framework of world politics.

The linkage doctrine has also been applied to a neighboring state, Angola, creating another obstacle to Namibia's independence. The issue here is that the United States and South Africa oppose the presence of Cuban troops in Angola, which is within its right as a sovereign state, and rejects the implementation of the United Nations plan until the Cuban forces are withdrawn. This is an interjection of the East-West conflict into southern African regional politics and, therefore, has had an impact on the foreign policies of the front-line states. As independent countries, the front-line states have developed relations with socialist countries such as China and Yugoslavia and those in Eastern Europe.

In accordance with the linkage doctrine, Angola could not be allowed to autonomy to conduct its own foreign policy, especially to negotiate treaties with countries outside the region that might oppose Western interests, including its invitation to Cuba for assistance in defending itself against South Africa. By making the Cuban troops in Angola an issue of the negotiations process, the United States and South Africa have attempted to shift the moral responsibility for Namibia's independence upon Angola. Thus Angola should pay for Namibian independence through a limitation of its sovereignty.

By linking the issue of Cuban troops in Angola to the Namibian question, the Reagan administration has intricated Namibian independence with the collective regional security of South Africa and the global East-West conflict. Since the Cuban revolution, successive American administrations have viewed this Caribbean island as a constant irritant in the Western hemisphere and its activities outside the region as evidence of Eastern bloc expansionism. American hostility toward Cuba intensified when Cuba, as chairman of the Non-Aligned Movement from 1976 to 1979, was an influential force in the third world and at the United Nations. In agreeing to the settlement of Namibia's independence within the framework of resolution 435 and at the same time introducing the "parallel" element of Cuban troops in Angola, the Reagan administration revealed that it was not seriously committed to the resolution of the Namibian question under the auspices of the United Nations and had doomed the implementation of resolution 435 to failure. By interjecting the East-West conflict through the issue of Angola and the removal of Cuban troops, the linkage doctrine was designed to fulfill two objectives at the same time. Firstly, it would destroy the legitimacy of Cuba. Secondly, it would delay the independence of Namibia and give South Africa time to reconstruct the territory on its own terms. Thus, from 1978 to the present, the world has seen the Namibian question become totally entangled in Cold War issues that have nothing to do with the independence of Namibia.

For most members of the global community, the Cuban troops issue is not just "extraneous," but false. In their view, since Angola invited the Cuban forces to assist them in their defense against South African attacks, the Cuban presence is an internal matter, within Angola's sovereign rights as an independent state, and is totally unrelated to negotiations over Namibia's independence.

The primary beneficiary of these complications and delaying tactics has been the apartheid system of South Africa. South Africa has been able to distract the attention of the world community from the real issue in southern Africa, the unjust and inhumane apartheid system. Thus the Pretoria government has been able to use the Namibian issue to avoid the growing conflict within South Africa itself and to enhance its standing at least among Western governments.

In the beginning, the initiatives of the Contact Group and resolution 435 brought some hope that Namibia's independence could be resolved in due course. But as the years have passed and negotiations have stalled, the self-serving motives of the Contact Group have been exposed. A global consensus now recognizes that the strategy of the Contact Group has only served to increase the status of an outcast regime that had been formerly isolated globally and to place the settlement plan outside of multilateral diplomacy. Thus the policy of "constructive engagement" between the United States and South Africa and the introduction of the linkage doctrine into the Namibian question by the Contact Group under the leadership of the United States have severely complicated the resolution of the issue: they are the major reasons for the postponement of Namibian independence.

The efforts of the Contact Group to secure Namibian independence, however, have begun to break down, and their "good offices" have been harshly questioned. At the Paris international conference in 1983, the world community reasserted its demand that the negotiations process be returned to the auspices of the United Nations. The conference also saw the first member of the Contact Group publicly distance itself from the linkage doctrine which has encumbered and delayed the negotiations. We thus begin to see the formation of a new global consensus in support of Namibia's independence.

4: The United Nations and the Return to Multilateral Diplomacy

The Paris Conference

The UN Council for Namibia, with the staunch backing of the Non-Aligned Movement, held an International Conference in Support of the Struggle of the Namibian People for Independence in Paris, April 25–29, 1983. The purpose was to provide the global community with an opportunity to review and assess the work of the Contact Group. The international community had become convinced since 1978 that a solution for Namibia was imminent. Indeed, at all international forums the Contact Group had pleaded for moderation and asked the nations of the world to give it the time and opportunity to implement Security Council resolution 435. A number of countries, led by the United Kingdom, had argued that the "constructive engagement" policy of the Reagan administration should be given a chance to work. France, too, was an active participant in the process, and the election of a socialist government in France appeared to be an additional assurance to the supporters of the UN resolutions, and particularly to SWAPO, that their interests would not be betrayed.

The Paris conference was a turning point in the negotiations for Namibia's independence, for the following reasons:

- SWAPO took the initiative in persuading the international community that the Contact Group's activities were proving to be counterproductive.
- The Council for Namibia, in its preparatory documents, clearly revealed the military strategy of South Africa and the economic and social consequences of this military strategy for the Namibian people.
- The Non-Aligned Movement, the Organization of African Unity, and the front-line states came to the Paris conference with a common strategy to insist that the negotiations for Namibia's independence be brought back to the United Nations and conducted through multilateral diplomacy.
- The linkage doctrine, or parallelism, whereby the removal of Cuban troops from Angola is made a precondition for negotiating the independence of Namibia, was discredited and declared extraneous.
- France, a member of the Contact Group, publicly began to disassociate itself from the position of the Contact Group, especially over the linkage doctrine advocated by the U.S. government, signaling the beginning of the breakup of the Contact Group initiative.

The president of SWAPO, Sam Nujoma, opened the Paris conference by exposing the efforts of the Contact Group and the strategy of South Africa and stressing that these activities served to delay Namibian independence. He pointed out that, after a brief euphoria over the Contact Group proposal, South Africa had used the time since 1978 to undermine the efforts of the United Nations by linking the question of Namibian independence with other crisis points in the world system. He stated emphatically:

The negative developments which have continued to impede progress towards Namibia's independence in the course of the last three years reflect the overall negative developments on the world scene. It is sad but proper and necessary to state here . . . that the past three years have seen the resurgence of the ugly cold-war-mongering, reactionary policies of confrontations, threats of intervention and intensified covert activities against progressive governments and, above all, the most dangerous threat of nuclear holocaust by the aggressive circles of imperialism.[38]

He asked the conference to examine the real motives of the countries involved in the Contact Group. President Nujoma named the countries that were either covertly or openly supporting the

South African regime. By doing so, he no doubt alienated certain Western European countries who had hoped that such references would be omitted and that they could avoid their responsibilities.

The most important part of his speech was the directive given to him by the Central Committee of SWAPO on the role of the Contact Group.

In this connection, I have been mandated by the Central Committee of SWAPO to categorically and clearly state that our Movement, having reviewed the history of the negotiations and the role of the so-called Contact Group, led by the United States, has concluded that this Group has lost proper contact with the letter and spirit of resolution 435 (1978) and that the whole exercise has now turned out to be a mere rescue operation for the white racist, illegal occupiers in Namibia. In particular, the Central Committee of SWAPO has singled out the Reagan Administration which, because of its public embrace of *apartheid* South Africa, has injected into the decolonization process of our country, an extraneous issue by linking the independence of Namibia to a withdrawal of Cuban forces from the People's Republic of Angola. The Central Committee categorically rejected and vehemently condemned this unjust, arrogant, and irrational and objectionable policy of linkage. The position of SWAPO is that the oppressed people of Namibia are entitled to independence without any further delay, pre-condition or prevarication.

It is in the light of this that SWAPO has come to the conclusion that the role of the five Western powers has ceased to be that of honest brokers in terms of the implementation of Security Council resolution 435 (1978). These Powers, and the Reagan Administration, in particular, must be prevailed upon to desist forthwith from their sinister attempts to hijack and misuse the Namibian negotiating process for their own selfish ends.[39]

The speech was significant in at least two other areas. President Nujoma explained that internal developments within SWAPO were not to be used by other countries to destabilize the movement. There was to be no question of the legitimacy of SWAPO as the sole and authentic representative of the Namibian people. He was responding to the objection of some Western countries to SWAPO's leadership and to their objective of reducing SWAPO to one constituent element in Namibia that would, at best, form a coalition government with other groupings, especially those supported by the Turnhalle Alliance. The inclusion of other groupings has been a South African strategy to institutionalize a tribal/racial representative political system in Namibia. This policy had been rejected by the vast majority of countries at the United Nations, and they were in no mood to compromise on the subject in Paris. (There was a feeble attempt by South Africa and its allies to send a representative of the Turnhalle Alliance to the conference. This individual registered as a visitor and proceeded to lobby for this position at the conference. His role, however, was quickly exposed, and he was barred from participating in the conference proceedings.)

What is often misunderstood about SWAPO's claim as sole and authentic representative is that it is not based merely on the fact that the majority of the people in Namibia support SWAPO. Like other liberation movements, SWAPO is self-consciously a multi-tribal and nonracial organization with an international perspective. Most nations of Africa, Asia, Latin America, and the Caribbean are well aware that tribalism and communalism can destroy a nation after independence. Hence, in order to insure that Namibia will not be subdivided by secessionist movements once it is independent, they too have insisted that there can be only one representative of the Namibian people. Secondly, the vast majority of countries are aware that negotiations with South Africa for Namibian independence should not be confused with the process adopted by ex-British colonies when they negotiated with Great Britain for a Westminster or *ministerial* type of model government. SWAPO is involved in a war of national liberation. Its adversary, the Republic of South Africa, must come to a military settlement as well as a constitutional settlement. Under these circumstances, President Nujoma made it known, SWAPO's representation and status were not up for negotiation.

The president of the Council for Namibia, Ambassador Paul Lusaka, also stated that the Council and the UN system were not going to be circumvented by the Contact Group initiative. In a hard-hitting statement, he identified the coalition that South Africa was developing and assessed their strategy for delaying Namibian independence:

With alarming indifference to universally held principles of morality, justice and freedom some Western States had aided and abetted Pretoria's diabolical schemes and had remained oblivious to the carnage it was perpetrating among the peace-loving peoples of southern Africa in general and Namibia in particular. . . .

Of late, with the active support of the United States, South Africa has held hostage the inalienable right of the Namibian people to self-determination and independence by injecting an outmoded and discredited cold-war rhetoric and by engaging in machinations intended to distort the nature of the question of Namibia and give it a dimension contrary to that of the act of colonial domination violating the principles and objectives of the Charter and decisions and resolutions of the United Nations. More specifically, South Africa and the United States had continued in their attempts to link the question of Namibia with irrelevant and extraneous questions such as the presence of Cuban forces in Angola, an issue unrelated to the United Nations plan and which fell under the exclusive competence of the Government of Angola.[40]

The claims of the Contact Group that Namibian independence had to be linked to the withdrawal of Cuban forces from Angola, he argued, were inadmissible. Angola had the right to develop its own foreign policy objectives, and no country or group of countries should interfere in the internal affairs of an independent African state.

The position taken by the foreign minister of France, Claude Cheysson, proved to be an important development of the conference. He began by justifying France's continued participation in the Contact Group and pointed out that while some progress had been made the time had come to move forward, since the earlier objectives were already achieved. He explained:

The group has now completed its work. The three-stage plan elaborated in September 1981 to restore the confidence among the parties to the conflict was accepted by the latter after long negotiations during which the front-line countries and above all SWAPO, the organization primarily concerned, displayed a spirit of compromise and honesty which I am pleased to stress here, following the examples of others. Everything is therefore ready for implementing resolution 435 (1978) and the settlement plan of the Security Council.[41]

Then in a surprising move, Cheysson began to distance his government from the Contact Group on the question of Cuban forces. In an obvious reference to Angola and the issue of Cuban troops, he insisted that the continued introduction of new conditions into the negotiations process was becoming unacceptable to France:

It could then have been thought that Namibia would accede rapidly to independence following free elections under international supervision. That did not happen because other problems, other requirements and other pretexts were advanced.

France cannot accept this. I do not suppose that anyone in this hall will accept it.

This blunt affirmation which, I have no doubt, will be criticized, does not mean that France is unaware of the difficulties and problems which will arise following independence, or that it is indifferent to them. It means, however, that resolutions cannot be obstructed by other considerations. As was noted recently by the United Nations Commissioner for Namibia, it is not acceptable that the Namibian people should serve as a hostage to force neighbouring countries to take up other matters, however important they may be.[42]

The general debate that followed the opening statements of the president of SWAPO, the president of the Council for Namibia, and the foreign minister of France, provided the framework for the rest of the speeches. The newly elected chairperson of the Non-Aligned Movement, Prime Minister Indira Gandhi of India, the secretary-general of the OAU, and representatives of Asia, Africa, and Latin America, the majority of which are non-aligned countries, reiterated their support, especially for the objectives stated by SWAPO. Having achieved a consensus on the issue earlier within their own meetings, non-aligned countries were able to present a unified position in support of SWAPO. They also argued that the introduction of the linkage doctrine and the role of the Contact Group were serving as obstructions to the UN plan. A number of European states also associated themselves with some of SWAPO's objectives. While some Western countries, notably those in the Contact Group, did not actively participate in the conference, many smaller countries of Western Europe were well represented. Several, including the Netherlands, Norway, Austria, and Ireland, indicated that they were not in complete agreement with the linkage concept and argued for the implementation of resolution 435 without this red herring.

The socialist countries that participated actively in the conference also indicated their strong support for positions taken by SWAPO, the Council for Namibia, the NAM, the OAU, and the front-line states. Most of the socialist countries were particularly alarmed that the southern Africa region was becoming dangerously embroiled in the East-West conflict with the possibility of a nuclear confrontation.

The vast majority of the nongovernmental organizations present also joined in the global consensus. Their views are best summarized by Abdul Minty, chief rapporteur of the 1980 International Conference in Solidarity with the Struggle of the People of Namibia, in a background paper presented to the Paris conference. He explained how the linkage concept had been slipped into the negotiations process and how it had been universally rejected—with the major exception of the United States:

> ... Representatives of the Five [Contact Group] visited Africa from 7–12 June [1982] and it was during this visit that an entirely new element was introduced into the negotiations. Most of the "points" concerned the items which had previously been identified as needing to be resolved ie. the cease-fire, UN impartiality and UNTAG. However, a new heading appeared which read "Other Regional Issues." This referred to other longstanding problems of the region at present hindering the development of the climate of securities and mutual confidence necessary for a Namibian settlement.
>
> This heading was widely regarded as referring to "linkage" ie. the insistence by the United States of "linking" the withdrawal of Cuban forces from Angola to the implementation of the UN plan for Namibia. For the first time an issue which had until then been a purely bilateral matter between the United States and the People's Republic of Angola had been formally introduced into the Namibian negotiations. (The United States has refused to establish diplomatic relations with Angola until Cuban forces have been withdrawn; all other members of the Contact Group maintain diplomatic relations with Angola.)
>
> Such "linkage and parallelism" has been rejected not only by SWAPO and the People's Republic of Angola but by the Front-Line States, the OAU, the Non-Aligned Summit, the UN General Assembly and the UN Secretary-General himself. Moreover to varying degrees the other members of the Contact Group, apart from the United States, have made it clear that they do not believe that the withdrawal of Cuban forces can be made into a pre-condition for a Namibian settlement.[43]

The discussions at the Paris conference were also greatly influenced by three documents prepared by the UN Council for Namibia. The first document was a detailed description of economic conditions in Namibia. It concluded that Western economic interests were largely responsible for the underdevelopment of Namibia and that they controlled much of the territory's economy, as follows:

The foreign economic interests involved in the exploitation of Namibian resources included many of the world's largest corporations and financial institutions from South Africa, Western Europe, and North America. The latest available information indicates that there are as many as 88 transnational corporations operating in Namibia, of which 35 are based in South Africa, 25 in the United Kingdom, 15 in the United States, 8 in the Federal Republic of Germany, 3 in France and 2 in Canada. All of these corporations, including those registered in South Africa, conduct their operations by means of licences issued by the colonial Pretoria regime or its illegal administration in Namibia. In 1981 alone, more than 250 licences for mineral prospecting in Namibia were approved by the illegal South African administration.

The importance of Namibia to South Africa and other economic interests is considerable.... Five of South Africa's six mining finance houses, as well as other Western economic interests, have extensive interests in diamonds, base metals and uranium exploration and production. The fishing industry is controlled by six South African companies and a seventh company is involved in the white fish and trawling sector. Banking and insurance companies based in South Africa, the United Kingdom, France and the Federal Republic of Germany control almost all banking and general financial activities in the private sector.[44]

The study drew from the extensive findings of the earlier hearings on Namibian uranium held by the Council for Namibia which revealed the connections between South African corporations and corporations located within Contact Group countries in the illegal mining of Namibian uranium. The conference was thus reminded of how South Africa and the Contact Group were using Namibian uranium to develop nuclear power, with the possibility of creating nuclear weapons. Not only was this exploitation of Namibian uranium in violation of Decree No. 1 for the Protection of the Natural Resources of Namibia, but its misuse endangered the region and the world. The study came to the conclusion that by allowing these transnational corporations to operate freely in Namibia the Western countries involved were directly responsible for bolstering South African control over the territory. Thus, not only is Namibia politically important to the Pretoria government, but South Africa is also dependent upon the territory for a number of minerals essential to its national security. Furthermore, the Contact Group countries have more than a passing interest in supporting the Pretoria government because of the investments of its transnational corporations in Namibia.

The second document graphically described the social conditions of the Namibian people. For example:

The Namibian labour force is divided along racial lines by the *apartheid* regime. Discrimination exists in the work situation, in wages, in the right to organize in trade unions and the types of jobs available to the different races.

The vast majority of black Namibians have become dependent on wage labour for survival. The total black work force is estimated at 481,000 of whom 240,000 are engaged in unproductive subsistence agriculture and 241,000 are employed in the white-owned sectors of the economy. Nearly all black Namibians are dependent on the wages earned by this second group.[45]

Details were also given on the lack of health and safety conditions for Namibians in the uranium mining sectors as well as the damage being done to the environment. The conference was reminded of the tragic consequences for the social development of the Namibian people if they continued in this illegal subjugated relationship with the apartheid government of South Africa.

The third document described the military aspects of the Namibian crisis and in so doing raised the question as to whether South Africa was at all interested in giving Namibia its independence. It noted that one of South Africa's military objectives was to integrate itself with the Western alliance system. It provided details as to how South Africa's dual military strategy in the region, i.e., the destabilization of front-line states and the military occupation of Namibia and parts of Angola, served the purpose of delaying Namibia's independence. The UN document explained the consequences of this military strategy for the countries of southern Africa in the following:

In its escalating war against the people of Namibia and South Africa and their national liberation movements, SWAPO and the African National Congress of South Africa (ANC), the racist regime of South Africa has also subjected Botswana, Lesotho, Mozambique, Seychelles, Zambia and Zimbabwe to subversion, military aggression, incursions and other destabilization tactics. As part of its conspiracy against these African States, South Africa has been recruiting, training, financing and equipping mercenaries to cause instability and supplied dissident groups with military hardware and funds in their attacks against the legitimate Governments of these States. According to press sources, a large number of "puppets" from Zambia, Zimbabwe and Mozambique have been trained to act against the Governments of their respective countries.[46]

The conference then strongly denounced South Africa's activities in Namibia and the entire region of southern Africa as a threat to global peace and security. Once again the Republic of South Africa found itself completely isolated. Nearly 130 countries called for an early meeting of the Security Council with the express purpose of imposing sanctions against South Africa. This, they argued, was the only way South Africa would comply with the resolutions and decisions of the United Nations. The conference expressed specific concern about the ability of South Africa to develop nuclear weapons and thus blackmail the rest of the world, especially its neighboring states, into subservience. Fearful that the continued exploitation of Namibian resources would leave the people and the country impoverished upon independence, the declaration of the Paris conference also noted that South African and foreign economic interests should be made responsible for paying reparations to an independent government in Namibia, once South Africa had removed itself from the territory.

Finally, the Paris declaration accepted the suggestion made by President Nujoma of SWAPO at the outset of the conference that the time had come for the Contact Group to either deliver or remove itself from the negotiations process. The Contact Group members themselves were beginning to raise questions, especially with regard to the linkage doctrine introduced by the United States. Canada had always been a reluctant partner. Great Britain and the Federal Republic of Germany were gradually distancing themselves from a hard-line position. And now, at the Paris conference, France openly disagreed with the linkage doctrine. It was clear that almost the entire global community rejected the complication of the negotiations process with the issue of Cuban troops in Angola. Thus only two countries stand in the way of implementing resolution 435—the United States and South Africa. In light of the failure of the Contact Group to make any significant progress over the years, the vast majority of those present at the international conference concluded that the question of Namibia's independence should be taken back to the United Nations. The conference was of the opinion that it was the responsibility of the United States to convince South Africa to negotiate in good faith with the United Nations. and SWAPO to implement resolution 435.

The UN Security Council Debates

There was a flurry of activities at the United Nations around the Namibian question during 1983 and early 1984. At the May 23–28, 1983, Security Council meetings a large number of foreign ministers from the front-line states, the OAU, and the NAM addressed the body. In addition, the United Nations heard from members of the Contact Group who had not participated in the Paris conference. These meetings made note of the fact that the secretary-general had made a number of initiatives to get the negotiations moving, but found that his efforts were thwarted by the intransigence of South Africa. President Sam Nujoma of SWAPO, who had not attended the United Nations for almost twelve years, made a statement before the Security Council reiterating, in stronger terms, what he had said at the Paris conference with regard to the activities of the Contact Group.

...SWAPO has come to the conclusion that the role of the five Western Powers has ceased to be that of an honest broker in terms of the implementation of Security Council resolution 435 (1978). These Powers, and the Reagan Administration in particular, must be prevailed upon to desist forthwith from their sinister attempts to hijack and misuse the Namibian negotiating process in their own economic and strategic interests.[47]

The representative of the Republic of South Africa made evident the attitude of his government toward SWAPO, the Security Council and the United Nations, when he stated:

It was not South Africa which created well-founded doubts in the minds of the people of the Territory concerning the United Nations bias in favour of SWAPO. It was the United Nations itself through the massive material, political and propaganda assistance which it extended—and indeed continues to extend—to SWAPO. Indeed this very meeting of the Security Council is a cynical demonstration of the United Nations bias in favour of SWAPO.[48]

Once again, South Africa placed the Namibian question in the context of its own regional security and the East-West conflict. Quoting his foreign minister, the South African representative defended the linking of the Cuban troops issue to Namibia's independence, using the language of the "Superpowers thesis":

There is an unquestionable *de facto* linkage between the withdrawal of Cuban forces from Angola and the settlement of the South West African question. It is ludicrous to suggest that the introduction of the hostile and expansionist surrogates of a super-powers into the southern African region will not have the most far-reaching implications for the security of all of the countries of the region, particularly when one considers:

(1) the doctrine of the super-power, the Soviet Union, which openly proclaims the necessity for the world-wide exportation of communism;
(2) the record of the surrogate Cuba, for subversion and the fomentation of revolution in Central America, South America and Africa;
(3) the threat which Soviet and Cuban supported elements have already posed to a country in the region, i.e., the Shaba invasion of Zaire.[49]

Mrs. Kirkpatrick, the U.S. ambassador, continued to support the work of the Contact Group and to defend its effort to reduce the points of disagreement between the parties. It was left to the alternate American representative, Mr. Lichenstein, to re-emphasize that the Reagan administration was determined to pursue the linkage doctrine:

... If there is to be a lasting settlement we need to create the conditions in which all countries in the region most particularly South Africa and Angola—can feel secure and turn their energies to their own development. This would of necessity involve not only complete respect for territorial integrity by all countries within the region; it must also involve the withdrawal of all foreign forces in the region. Creating the security conditions that in turn may provide a climate of confidence will be an essential part of this settlement which we all devoutly wish and towards which we are all earnestly working.[50]

In response to the position of South Africa and the United States, Mr. Nujoma was highly critical of the persistent efforts of the South African government and the Contact Group to remove the Namibian question from the United Nations and to insist on the inclusion of other matters:

... We strongly deplore the fact that, despite the unanimous adoption of the latest resolution of the Security Council, which *inter alia*, unambiguously reinforces the mandate of the United Nations Secretary-General as the principal authority in the implementation of resolution 435 (1978), the so-called contact group should still display the arrogance of power by deciding to hold another of its secret meetings on Namibia on 9 and 10 June in Paris, in order to further its members' deceptive manoeuvres and intrigues.

This development, coming as it does immediately after the end of this meeting, is diversionary and, in our view, destructive of the provisions of the latest resolution of the Council.

On our part, we most resolutely condemn and reject any attempt on the part of those countries further to complicate the Namibian issue by introducing dangerous and objectionable notions such as so-called general security considerations or other regional problems in southern Africa. Whether used euphemistically or explicitly, linkage in any form at all is totally repugnant and unacceptable to us and to the African people.[51]

At the October meetings of the Security Council, members examined the detailed report presented by the secretary-general on his visit to South Africa. The secretary-general reminded the South African government that the United Nations could not accept any linkage as a precondition for the implementation of the UN plan for Namibia. It was not a matter contained in the UN resolutions nor was it within his mandate to discuss the Cuban troops issue.

He then described South Africa's position as given to him by its foreign minister:

...He confirmed that the position of the South African Government was that the one major issue still to be resolved was the withdrawal of the Cubans from Angola, on the understanding that they would not be replaced by any other hostile forces. He further stated that firm agreement would have to be reached on the fundamental requirements of Cuban withdrawal and a commitment would have to be obtained from the Angolan Government regarding the implementation of such an agreement. The other outstanding issues, he stated, should be addressed and resolved within the framework of the understanding reached with the United States and the Western Contact Group.[52]

South Africa had now expanded its demands to include a settlement with Angola. Nonetheless, the secretary-general indicated that some progress had been made on the electoral system in Namibia and the role of the United Nations.

South Africa's defiance of the United Nations continued at the October Security Council meetings. Once again, the South African representative attacked the United Nations, especially certain units within it for accepting SWAPO as the "sole and authentic representative" of the Namibian people, and questioned the ability of the UN system to be an impartial observer of the electoral system.[53]

The SWAPO representative, reflecting the frustration of the vast majority of speakers, said that the time had come to challenge South Africa's refusal to move on the Namibian question and urged the Security Council to take other concrete actions. He thus recommended that the Security Council

impose comprehensive and mandatory sanctions under Chapter VII of the Charter against racist South Africa. It is our firm conviction that such historic action by the Council, which is the only remaining viable, realistic and peaceful means, will without doubt compel the Pretoria racist regime to co-operate fully in the speedy decolonization of Namibia on the basis of resolution 435 (1978).

What our people expect from this Council is a strong and unequivocal rejection of the linkage issue and a condemnation of the Washington-Pretoria unholy alliance which is responsible for it. We represent only a national liberation movement and a colonized people, whose yearning for freedom and daily suffering is the only justification for our struggle.[54]

Members of the Contact Group also participated in the October debates in the Security Council, and it is here that the major Western countries, with the exception of the United States, joined the global consensus in rebutting the linkage doctrine as an integral factor in the negotiations for the independence of Namibia. France was the most vociferous in its condemnation of the linkage doctrine and reinforced what it had said at the Paris conference and at the May Security Council meetings. The Canadian position was that "Namibia should have its independence regardless of what happens or what does not happen in Angola" and that "South Africa, cannot, however, legitimize its illegal occupation of Namibia by raising other issues."[55]

The representative of the Federal Republic of Germany distanced his government from the position of the Contact Group, stating:

We believe that the right of the Namibian people to self-determination and independence must be recognized and should be implemented irrespective of any other problem. During the last Council debate my delegation emphasized that this issue does not fall within the scope of the mission the contact group undertook in 1977.[56]

Finally, even Great Britain concluded that the Security Council should view Cuban troops in Angola and Namibian independence as "separate issues."[57] Only the United States refused to give up the linkage doctrine and took the position that much progress had been made and that South Africa had given up considerable ground.[58] Thus when the Security Council adopted resolution 539 on Namibia, parts of which rejected linkage as an extraneous issue "incompatible with resolution 435" and opposed the independence of Namibia being "held hostage to the resolutions of issues that are alien to Security Council 435," the vote was fourteen in favor, none opposed, and one abstention, belonging to the United States.

At the end of the October Security Council meetings, with the exception of the United States, South Africa was once again isolated in the international community. The global consensus achieved at the international conference in Paris with the support of the NAM and the OAU had gained new strength as members of the Contact Group disassociated themselves from the linkage issue as a precondition.

The General Assembly meetings on the question of Namibia followed the Security Council meetings and reiterated similar points. The views and frustrations of the General Assembly can best be summarized in the words of Indian delegate, Mr. Ramachandran:

Thirty-seven years have elapsed since the question of Namibia was first raised at the United Nations and 17 years since the General Assembly adopted resolution 2145 (XXI), which terminated the Mandate transmitted to South Africa by the League of Nations and placed the Territory under direct United Nations responsibility. For 16 years now Namibia has remained under the jurisdiction of its sole legal Administering Authority, the United Nations Council for Namibia. Twelve years ago the International Court of Justice, in a historic advisory opinion, held South Africa's occupation of Namibia to be illegal and deemed that South Africa was under an obligation to withdraw its administration immediately from Namibia. And, finally, five years ago the Security Council adopted the United Nations plan for the independence of Namibia, embodied in its resolution 435 (1978)...

We have learnt from the bitter experience of the last few years that optimism in the Namibian context is dangerous since it has led so far only to shattered hopes and expectations.[59]

He remained hopeful that with the adoption of resolution 539 (1983), there might be some movement on the issue.

In December 1983, Angola, which had recently been invaded again by South Africa, requested a Security Council meeting to seriously examine the motives of the government of South Africa. South Africa defended its attack on Angola as an attack against SWAPO. The South African representative also read a letter from his foreign minister to the secretary-general indicating his government's willingness to disengage its military operations against SWAPO in Angola if Angola would reciprocate.[60] The U.S. representative found this to be conciliatory and a positive step.[61]

The Angolan representative, on the other hand, appealed to the Security Council not to be misled by South Africa's offer:

Is this latest offensive commensurate with the sentiments expressed in the letter by the racist South African Foreign Minister to the Secretary-General? And will the Council once more allow itself to be duped by South Africa's wiles? Even a cursory reading of the letter reveals that in fact the racist regime has really made no offer at all; all that the letter contains is a vague statement that it is prepared to begin a disengagement, but it does not talk of withdrawal. Furthermore, it again brings up the issue of linkage, which the Government of Angola, supported by most nations of the world, rejects absolutely and categorically.[62]

In spite of the many debates at the United Nations during 1983 and the secretary-general's visit to the region, his final report in December stated his regret that there was no further progress in his discussions with South Africa.[63]

The following year was 1984, one hundred years after the first colonization of Namibia, and the world seemed to have reached an impasse on the question of Namibian independence. There were no major changes in the negotiations process in 1984. Near the end of the year, October 31–November 2, 1984, the UN Council for Namibia held a symposium on a Century of Heroic Struggle of the Namibian People Against Colonial Occupation. In spite of the efforts of the global community including members of the Contact Group, the Republic of South Africa has chosen to resist the efforts of the United Nations to bring about independence for Namibia.

The Price of "Constructive Engagement"

For the people of Namibia, what was initially a peaceful multilateral negotiations procedure to secure their independence has been gradually transformed into a confrontational bilateral stalemate. Only South Africa and the United States remain opposed to SWAPO's and the global community's pursuit of negotiations for Namibia's independence under the auspices of the United Nations.

Acting in concert, and against the global consensus of the United Nations, the United States and South Africa have complicated and obstructed the implementation of the UN plan. Not only have these two governments attempted to hijack the Namibian issue outside the UN system, but they have enveloped Namibia's independence in the tensions of the new Cold War. This forebodes real dangers for the peoples of Africa and the entire world inasmuch as the Republic of South Africa has recently joined the group of nuclear states.

The Reagan policy of "constructive engagement" has effectively involved all of southern Africa in the politics of the new Cold War and turned it into an arena of conflict. South Africa believed that by adopting a strategy of diplomacy (delaying negotiations), politics (supporting dissident groups), economics (manipulating movements of labor and capital), and direct military invasions, it could create a *cordon sanitaire* along its borders that would guarantee its security and allow it to continue its apartheid policies. Namibia was the key element in this grand design. The postponement of Namibian independence then became a permanent and critically important feature of South Africa's foreign policy.

Though the Namibian people have paid the highest price, "constructive engagement" has been costly in other areas. The policy has had a serious impact on the principle and role of multilateral decision-making. The UN system, including its many agencies, is now under massive attack by those who propose to destroy multilateral diplomacy and cripple the input of third-world countries in global decision-making. This attack was preceded by efforts to destroy regional coalitions, such as the front-line states, continental coalitions, such as the OAU, and international coalitions, such as the Non-Aligned Movement. Early on, the Reagan administration informed third-world countries that it would monitor the votes of the UN General Assembly and punish those states opposed to U.S. interests. Many countries that are heavily indebted because of U.S. foreign aid and loans are therefore reluctant to exercise their sovereignty, and, in effect, have become client states of the United States. Reeling from this assault on multilateral diplomacy, the United Nations has responded weakly. However, with the Namibian question, it has an opportunity to resurrect itself.

There is a great deal of third-world disenchantment with the UN effort to implement resolution 435. The United Nations has three bodies to deal with the Namibian question: the Council for Namibia, which acts as a legislative body; the commissioner, who acts as an executive officer; and a special representative who acts as a negotiating authority. The Council for Namibia should expand its legislative powers and be more forceful in de-legitimizing the illegal regime in Namibia. In its ten-year history, the Council has passed one decree, and it has yet to be implemented. Furthermore, the Council has allowed itself to be maneuvered out of the negotiations process by a third party, the Contact Group, which has no legitimate role in the proceedings. A renewed assertion of the role of the Council for Namibia should pose little difficulty since the Council has the backing of the global community at the United Nations.

The global community is in agreement that the negotiations for Namibia's independence should be brought back to the United Nations and resolved through a multilateral process. If there is to be a negotiated and peaceful settlement of the Namibian question, it becomes necessary for all the parties involved to return to the negotiating table under the auspices of the United Nations, the only organization that enjoys universal legitimacy. The bilateral process as outlined by South Africa and the United States would only prolong the armed struggle in the region, seriously affecting the fabric of Namibian society and increasing tensions between the major powers.[64]

The thirty-ninth General Assembly, meeting in the fall of 1984, was the scene of a major confrontation between the United States and the Non-Aligned Movement. Led by Ambassador Kirkpatrick, the United States sought to water down the resolution that had been carefully drafted by the NAM in conjunction with SWAPO by introducing a number of amendments. This was denied by Ambassador Noel Sinclair of Guyana, who insisted that the rules of procedure of the General Assembly stipulated that items relating to Namibia had to be deemed "substantive," thus requiring a two-thirds majority of the General Assembly (Rule 84). Through this parliamentary maneuver, the non-aligned were able to preserve the integrity of their position and resist efforts to weaken it. Once again, this maneuver revealed to members of the movement the importance of working in close coordination with one another at the United Nations if they are to preserve their principles. While the non-aligned countries won a major victory, it should be remembered that, shortly afterward, the movement fell hopelessly into disarray over the amendments on apartheid. Here the United States was able to use parliamentary procedures to delay and gain time to lobby support and defeat the non-aligned position on apartheid.

These two issues, Namibia and apartheid, reveal quite dramatically the fundamental changes that have occurred in the United Nations. As we pointed out earlier, the United States has embarked on a policy of monitoring votes at the United Nations and punishing its enemies and rewarding its friends. The politics of coercion in international organizations has replaced the politics of persuasion. In an era where food has become a political weapon, all countries, but especially the non-aligned and other third-world countries, are forced to adapt painfully to this situation while attempting to maintain their sovereignty and integrity as independent states.

For the global community and especially the NAM, the Contact Group initiative has collapsed. In spite of the Contact Group's failure, the United States insists that its policy of "constructive engagement" with South Africa could result in the independence of Namibia. The United States has accepted the South African view that the only stumbling block for Namibian independence is the presence of Cuban troops in Angola. The February 21, 1985, hearings of the U.S. House Committee on African Affairs revealed that the Reagan administration had not fundamentally changed its position.

Assistant Secretary of State Chester Crocker, who has close contacts with the apartheid regime, reported at the February House Committee hearings that South Africa would withdraw all but

1,500 of the estimated 25,000 to 30,000 (others estimate 100,000) members of its occupation army in Namibia if Angola would agree to the withdrawal of Cuban troops immediately. After the remaining forces were removed simultaneously, elections would be held in Namibia according to the UN plan. However, this was a shift from a previous agreement between Angola and South Africa. Taking the South African and U.S. view at face value, the government of Angola in a dramatic gesture had presented a plan in November 1984 to withdraw 20,000 of the estimated 25,000 Cuban troops from Angola in stages over a three-year period. South Africa presented a similar proposal to withdraw its troops from Namibia. This would have begun the disengagement process.

The House Committee on African Affairs was startled then to learn in February from Crocker that South Africa is now insisting on parallel withdrawal, and negotiations have stalled once again. The reason South Africa gave for this new qualification is that Angola and Cuba threaten its security. Crocker and the Reagan administration have on previous occasions accepted the view that the security of the apartheid regime was paramount and could not be threatened by external forces. But it is Angola that has been invaded and attacked on several occasions by South Africa, and it therefore has even more to fear with regard to its security. This led Congressman Stephen Solarz of New York to remark at the February 21 hearing:

It's hard to me to understand how 5,000 Cuban troops above the 13th Parallel, some 1,700 kilometers from South Africa, and 500 kilometers from Namibia, would be a security threat to South Africa.[65]

The chairman of the House Committee on African Affairs, Mr. Howard Wolpe, challenged the assistant secretary's assessment of the situation:

There were invasions, but today there is a permanent continuing occupation of Angola. From an Angolan perspective I suspect that's not a heck of a lot of progress.

From the South African perspective they're sitting pretty well at this time.

Nothing you have said today offers any concrete evidence of change in the situation.[66]

Crocker's immediate response was to insist, "It's inappropriate for me to defend the position of either party,". adding that the United States was acting only as a "mediator."[67] He concluded pessimistically:

The negotiations for Namibia's independence have—like many multi-lateral negotiations, including the effort to end minority rule in Zimbabwe—been protracted, and this caused some to conclude that the effort is hopeless.[68]

This raises the question of how a country that does not have normal relations with one of the major participants, i.e., Cuba, can claim the moral legitimacy to engage in multilateral diplomacy, especially when it takes the view that the effort is "hopeless."

During the question-and-answer period, Crocker casually mentioned that the United States had decided to suspend the activities of its liaison unit in Windhoek and to monitor the situation from Johannesburg. Questions had been raised in the global community about the status in international law of a U.S. liaison unit in Namibia and its capacity to collect information about the territory when it is dependent on South Africa for transport and movement within Namibia. Earlier at these hearings, international lawyer Gay McDougall had provided considerable evidence questioning the legality of this unit.[69] The decision to suspend the activities of the liaison unit was a major victory for the NAM and SWAPO, both of whom had argued vehemently against it at the thirty-ninth General Assembly debates on the Namibian question.

The cost of "constructive engagement" has also been high for the front-line states, particularly Angola. Angola cannot be sanguine about the overtures of the South African government or about the "good offices" offered by the United States. For example, Angola is being asked by South Africa to police SWAPO in southern Angola as a price for South Africa's withdrawing its troops from Namibia, the launching pad for military strikes into Angola! This not only interferes with Angola's sovereignty as an independent state, infringing on its ability to conduct its own foreign relations, but also essentially holds the Namibian people hostage. Furthermore, Angola cannot provide this guarantee unless SWAPO and South Africa come to a cease-fire. In addition, South Africa has sought the inclusion of Jonas Savimbi as a member of the Angolan government and engages in a policy of leashing and unleashing Savimbi to disrupt domestic Angolan politics. Nonaligned countries have recalled that nearly three decades ago John Foster Dulles persistently challenged the legitimacy of the government of the People's Republic of China by leashing and unleashing Chiang Kai-shek as the authentic representative of the Chinese people. To preserve its sovereignty, Angola cannot accede to the demands of South Africa that it ask the Cuban troops to leave. If it should do this, Angola would become a proxy state and an integral part of the *cordon sanitaire* along the borders of South Africa that, in turn, would further institutionalize the apartheid system within South Africa. Taken all together, the NAM saw no prospect of Namibia's independence in the continuation of a policy of "constructive engagement." Consequently, they called for another extraordinary meeting at the ministerial level, to be held in New Delhi in April 1985.

5: The Non-Aligned Movement and the Legitimization of SWAPO

The New Delhi Extraordinary Meeting

The Co-ordinating Bureau of non-aligned countries held another extraordinary meeting on Namibia in New Delhi, April 19–21, 1985. This was an auspicious occasion, for April 19, 1985, marked the twenty-fifth anniversary of the founding of SWAPO. Yet, once again, South Africa defied the global community. On April 18, the day before the opening of the meeting, the South African government announced unilateral plans to establish an "interim government" in Namibia in clear violation of UN resolutions.

When the non-aligned ministers met, they faced the prospect of the total collapse of the Contact Group initiative and of the efforts of the United States to be either a conduit or mediator. The NAM has never viewed national liberation as hopeless. Its members have rejected the politics of postponement, i.e., creating illusions of the possibility of a negotiated settlement. They have categorically rejected the idea that the United Nations will no longer be an avenue of multilateral negotiations. They have also rejected the new concept of regional security devised by the United States for southern Africa, whereby weak states are clustered around a stronger state in the region and required to surrender their sovereignty to a designated regional power. As the dominant power in the region, the Republic of South Africa has become the local gendarme with full license to invade weaker states without fear of penalty. The non-aligned countries are fully aware that the strategy being implemented in southern Africa is being replicated in Central America, the Middle East, and other regions of the third world. They are reminded of the U.S. invasion of Grenada and the statement shortly afterward of the chief of South Africa's defense force, who used this event to justify his government's invasion of Angola. The non-aligned countries have rejected the West's notion of transforming southern Africa into a war zone to resolve the East-West conflict. Finally, the movement recognizes that the struggle for Namibian independence is structurally linked with the liberation movement of South Africa.

The host country, India, had prepared a draft statement and circulated it in New York at the United Nations prior to the New Delhi meeting, as is the custom of the NAM. In keeping with India's style, developed at the seventh summit, the draft was consciously designed for amplification at the formal meeting of the ministers. It addressed a number of ideological questions, but two issues were of primary concern: the role of the Contact Group, especially its relationship with the United Nations; and the dangers of the policy of "constructive engagement."

In New Delhi a number of hidden agenda items were also discussed in the anterooms of Vigyan Bhavan, the conference center. Firstly, there were the divisions among the front-line states, notably over maintaining a collective policy toward the South African government, as a number of states were beginning to develop bilateral relations with South Africa. Secondly, there was the question of the advisability of holding the forthcoming foreign ministers' meeting of non-aligned countries in Luanda, Angola, during September 1985. Given the military actions of South Africa and its surrogate Jonas Savimbi in the area, some countries had informally questioned the suitability of Luanda as the meeting place. Thirdly, there was the matter of the choice of the eighth summit site. The choice of the site of a non-aligned summit meeting, which is generally held every three years and which rotates from region to region, is significant, for the head of government of the host country serves as chairman of the movement until the next summit. When India assumed its chairmanship of the seventh summit in place of Iraq, which was involved in a war with Iran, it was understood that the eighth summit would then return to Baghdad. The unresolved Iran-Iraq war had made this possibility unlikely. In the light of these developments, a number of countries had begun to present their candidacies, and they used the occasion to lobby for their particular country.

Fourthly, there was the leadership of the new Indian prime minister, Rajiv Gandhi. The recent election had clearly established him as the successor to Mrs. Gandhi and the leader of India. This meeting was his first opportunity to appear as chairman of the NAM, and delegates were interested not only in observing his leadership qualities, but also in seeing whether India would depart from the policy of Mrs. Gandhi and Pandit Nehru. Over more than two decades of the NAM's existence, many delegates, especially foreign ministers, had developed close relationships with Mrs. Gandhi and a number of her advisors. The ministers were anxious to see whether the new prime minister would bring in other advisors and set new directions for the movement. In observing Rajiv Gandhi's changes in India's domestic sphere, the Western media, and particularly the *Wall Street Journal*, had dubbed his economic policies "Reaganomic." Hence there was some concern with whether the new prime minister was going to shift India's foreign policy from its traditional role as a non-aligned country to a more pro-Western position.

These hidden agenda items were dealt with immediately. Rajiv Gandhi made it clear at the outset that India's foreign policy was not a personal predilection of his mother or grandfather, but was rooted in Indian political institutions. Non-alignment was the foreign policy of India. It was an integral part of the Congress Party and, indeed, all the political parties of India, and was fixed within the administrative and cultural apparatuses of Indian society. Consequently, there had been no public discussion of an alternative foreign policy during the recent Indian election. In his opening speech, the prime minister reiterated India's traditional commitment to non-alignment and his determination to follow an independent foreign policy. This independent foreign policy of non-alignment was clearly displayed when he extended full diplomatic status to SWAPO (see below).

The other hidden agenda items were also quickly resolved. There was no public debate at the meeting on the Angola site. The Bureau concluded that a change of venue would be viewed as a defeat for the movement and a victory for South Africa. The argument that similar circumstances—a war situation—had prompted a change of venue from Baghdad to New Delhi for the seventh summit conference of non-aligned countries did not apply. In the case of the seventh summit, the shift to New Delhi was the result of a conflict between two non-aligned countries, Iraq and Iran. But in the case of Luanda, the conflict is between the government of South Africa and he entire non-aligned world. The ministers therefore reaffirmed in their final declaration their commitment to holding the foreign ministers' meeting in Luanda. A number of them did hint in their speeches that they were aware of the efforts of the South African government and the Pretoria-backed UNITA dissident group in Angola, led by Savimbi, to destabilize the Luanda meeting.

The non-aligned ministers postponed the discussion on the site of the eighth summit conference. There are two possible approaches. The first is to follow the precedent set between the sixth and seventh Summits, when the then chair of the movement, Fidel Castro of Cuba, held extensive consultations with the members until the NAM arrived at a consensus on holding the summit in India. The second alternative is to discuss the matter in Luanda, and let the foreign ministers recommend a site. As the current chair of the NAM, India has been suggesting that it may follow the "consensus mechanism."

Throughout the meeting, Rajiv Gandhi displayed complete control of the machinery of foreign policy-making in India. The most significant achievement of the New Delhi meeting was the decision by the Indian prime minister to accord SWAPO full diplomatic status. This was carefully planned and established a new procedure both in the movement and in international politics. From its inception, the NAM has attempted to change the rules of the game of international diplomacy. These rules, the non-aligned countries have argued, were created by Europe and the United States and are a part of a process that has historically excluded the third world. The United Nations itself was a creation of the victors of World War II, wherein the bulk of the third world countries did not participate.

The Non-Aligned Movement came into being primarily as a coalition of independent ex-colonial developing states having a common set of principles and objectives for a peaceful and more just world order. Its members have tried to transform not only the United Nations, but the entire multilateral system of diplomacy to ensure that small and middle-sized developing countries can participate in global decision-making. The NAM's most specific contribution, and the one that has had a decisive impact in world politics, is its support for the role and legal status of national liberation movements.[70]

India's decision to give SWAPO full diplomatic status was based on important precedents within the movement. National liberation movements are welcomed with guest status and often hold observer status as provisional governments before being confirmed as full members. On a number of previous occasions, the non-aligned countries had recognized provisional governments as full members of the movement prior to their achieving complete and full independence with state power. They were Algeria, at the first summit in 1961; Angola, in 1964; Vietnam, in 1973; and Zimbabwe, in 1979.

In most cases, the national liberation movements were involved in anticolonial struggles for independence from a European power. And immediately after the national liberation movements obtained political independence, they were quickly admitted to the United Nations and became members of the global community. Vietnam presented other complications, in that it was not only an anticolonial war, but an anti-imperialist war between a liberation movement and a major world power that was attempting to impose its own chosen faction on the nation. It was the NAM that was primarily responsible for making the case for the legitimacy of national liberation movements internationally prior to their attaining independence, including their right to armed struggle against a recalcitrant colonial power, if necessary.

The NAM has also given international support and legitimacy to the PLO and SWAPO. Both were recognized as observers in 1973, with the PLO becoming a full member in 1975 and SWAPO in 1978. Further recognition was given to their struggles and statuses when the non-aligned countries consistently elected the PLO and SWAPO to serve on the Co-ordinating Bureau of the movement. The support that the NAM has given to the struggles of the Palestinian people through the PLO and the Namibian people through SWAPO has not been without cost. The non-aligned countries recognize that the opposition to their principles and activities and the distortion of their objectives in the Western media are due in large part to their position on national liberation, especially in the Middle East and southern Africa.

The special situations of the PLO and SWAPO have led the non-aligned countries to treat them both differently from the other national liberation struggles. Conventional views generally consider SWAPO and the PLO lacking in a territorial base that is a prerequisite for recognition as a nation-state. In the case of the PLO, the NAM has historically supported the rights of the Palestinian people according to the Charter of the United Nations and its many resolutions. This includes their rights to a homeland. For the non-aligned countries, the Palestinian question is not a refugee issue. Nor is it purely a colonial question. They have insisted that it is a situation where a whole people have been displaced from their land and a settler state created. The question was always treated as a special category, with the non-aligned countries recognizing the Palestinian National Council as the parliament of the Palestinian people and the PLO, which enjoys the status of a state with the NAM, as its executive arm. This legitimization of the PLO, however, is distinctly different from Western diplomatic practice, which under certain conditions recognizes a government-in-exile.

The case of SWAPO and Namibia is also different from the examples cited above. Though the Republic of South Africa had held a mandate over Namibia, it had been abrogated by the International Court of Justice, a decision reaffirmed by the United Nations. The United Nations thereafter created the Council for Namibia for the administration of Namibia until independence, a unit which the South African government has systematically ignored. South Africa has also imposed apartheid policies both within its own territory and within Namibia, a social system that has been deemed "criminal" by the United Nations according to the Charter. In summary, non-aligned countries and the United Nations view as illegal the Republic of South Africa's occupation and governance of Namibia, including its imposition of a system that is an international crime against humanity.

In its more recent declarations, the United Nations has recognized that a people struggling for its own self-determination has rights as a *people* and does not necessarily have to be a state to enjoy them. Thus the people of Namibia have a legal right to conduct an armed struggle against this illegal occupying power, especially since this power governs them through the racist or "criminal" system of apartheid. The people of Namibia could also appeal to other nations to assist them in their resistance. This right to challenge established authority is legitimized by the fact that the movements for national liberation seek armed assistance from other states to challenge established authority (GA Declaration on the Principles of International Law Regarding Friendly Relations and Co-operation Amongst States, resolution 2625).

The Non-Aligned Movement has struggled for nearly a quarter of a century to provide legitimacy to a *people* and the *movement* which represents them decisively. This procedure of granting rights to a movement or a people before they possess territory or a state establishes a new practice in international politics. The unique role of national liberation movements in world politics has been distinctly defined by SWAPO in the following:

National liberation movements are not always easy to characterise. Unlike political parties they are bodies which express not class or sectional interests but national ones, under conditions where these have been undermined by foreign conquest, domination or occupation. A national liberation movement holds together supporters from all sectors of the population—men and women, young and old, peasants, intellectuals and workers—forged into a cohesive whole in pursuit of the goal of national independence.[71]

While a national liberation movement is a social movement of an entire population, SWAPO has a clear understanding that this is merely the beginning. A movement must also develop a precise organizational structure to enable it to become a legitimate political actor in the international system. Again SWAPO describes this structure as follows:

But mere mass support is not in itself enough. A sound organisational structure, a democratic decision-making process and a clear political understanding of the root economic structures and causes of oppression are vital to ensure that the movement does not become a loose populist one whose leaders could at some future time manipulate the masses. For true liberation, the attainment of state power is only the beginning. Africa has learnt to its cost that merely to unite national forces to get rid of a colonial power is not enough, because the structures of exploitation on which colonial domination is built have been systematically and deeply embedded in the colonised society.[72]

This definition of a national liberation movement allows for the possibility that a movement could be formed even within independent states. It is this phenomenon that is emerging in Central and Latin America, where national liberation movements have appeared to challenge the authority of military juntas and neo-colonial governments.

The United Nations system, by recognizing liberation movements within its body and giving them a right to sit in the various organs of that institution, has provided further legitimacy. As far as the global community is concerned, SWAPO presently enjoys this status and has the right to be the sole and authentic representative of the people of Namibia through the UN Council for Namibia, its legal administrative body until Namibia is independent. Furthermore, as we have noted earlier in this paper, Security Council resolutions 385 and 435 declared the Republic of South Africa an illegal administrator of Namibia who must negotiate the future status of Namibia with SWAPO.

These factors together led the Indian government at the New

Delhi extraordinary meeting to push the international community a little further by advancing the case for SWAPO's deserving full diplomatic status by the nation-states of the world. In according full diplomatic status to SWAPO, India was establishing the precedent that, in its view, SWAPO had territorial rights within Namibia that could not be negotiated by the government of South Africa. Prime Minister Rajiv Gandhi announced this innovative suggestion at the meeting:

South West Africa People's Organization is the sole, authentic representative of the Namibian people. It must receive greater political support as well as more tangible material assistance in pursuing its struggle. Today we observe the 25th anniversary of the establishment of South West Africa People's Organization. All of us must demonstrate our solidarity with South West Africa People's Organization through concrete pledges of assistance to the Non-Aligned Solidarity Fund for the Liberation of Namibia. India on its part will make a further contribution to the Fund. *I am glad to announce that the Government of India has decided to accord full diplomatic status to the South West People's Organization representative in New Delhi.*[73]

The example set by India has led a number of other non-aligned countries to follow suit.

At New Delhi, the foreign ministers were moved to issue a special communiqué on South Africa's unilateral attempt to create a puppet regime in Namibia.

This maneouvre by the racist regime of South Africa to install a so-called "internal administration" in Namibia constitutes the most brazen defiance of the United Nations, in particular, the Security Council, which declared in its resolution 439 (1978) that any unilateral measure taken by the illegal occupation regime in Namibia is null and void. This illegal action has evoked universal disapproval.

Since the General Assembly revoked South Africa's mandate over Namibia nearly two decades ago, the Pretoria regime had been consistently demonstrating its intention to impose an "internal solution" in Namibia in utter disregard of the demands of the Namibian people for self-determination and genuine independence and of the will of the international community.[74]

In this manner, the non-aligned countries were also calling upon the United Nations to act on these violations of resolution 439.

The non-aligned countries expanded the initial Indian draft and issued a final declaration on Namibia that was more militant than those issued previously by the movement. Three items deserve special mention. The first was the insistence of the Non-Aligned Movement that the matter of Namibia's independence be returned to the United Nations as the only outside authority to determine the future of Namibia and that the UN plan must be implemented.

The responsibility of the United Nations for the independence of Namibia must once again be strongly affirmed. Proposals by South Africa to push the role of the United Nations to the background must be resisted. This gathering of the Non-Aligned Movement proclaims that Namibian independence is the direct obligation of the United Nations. The Security Council must seek new ways to enforce resolution 435 (1978). That resolution remains the only acceptable basis for a peaceful settlement of the question of Namibia. We oppose any effort to by-pass the United Nations and promote spurious schemes of internal settlement.[75]

The Reagan administration and its policy of "constructive engagement" and the South African government and its policies were also condemned for the role they were playing in obstructing and undermining the UN plan.

The Bureau is convinced that the policy of so-called "constructive engagement" with South Africa, being pursued by the current United States Administration is in principle aimed at and is in fact strengthening and giving encouragement to the racist regime and that the regime's deepening intransigence, continued aggressive policy, and blackmail against neighbouring independent states, are reinforced by that Administration's "constructive engagement" policy. It urges that this policy, which has come under sharp criticism from several quarters, including within the United States itself, be abandoned.

The Bureau is gratified that the Movement of Non-Aligned Countries has continued to maintain a consensus on its determination to oppose any attempt to subvert the United Nations plan for the immediate independence of Namibia. In the face of South Africa's obvious challenge to the international community it has become even more urgent for the Non-Aligned Movement to intensify its efforts. The Extraordinary Ministerial Meeting presents a timely opportunity for all members of the

Movement to implement faithfully all its decisions on Namibia especially with respect to the diplomatic isolation of *apartheid* South Africa.[76]

The second issue that the Bureau stressed was the essential need to protect the Namibian and Angolan peoples, including their sovereignty, from the military aggression of South Africa.

The Bureau expresses its indignation at and condemns the reported new military offensive launched by South Africa on a massive scale in northern Namibia, under the code name "Operation Iron Fist." This new development must be seen as part of Pretoria's continuing designs to suppress Namibians through brute force, a strategy doomed to failure. The Bureau also expresses its grave concern at reports regarding the massing of South African forces in northern Namibia and the parts of Southern Angola occupied by South Africa, presaging another possible act of massive aggression against, and the destabilization of, the People's Republic of Angola.[77]

Thirdly, the movement once again decisively rejected the linkage concept inserted by the United States and South Africa into the negotiations process.

The Bureau once again condemns the linking by the USA and South Africa of the implementation of SCR 435 to elements extraneous to the independence of Namibia. Such linking has the objective of distorting the question of the independence of Namibia and of artificially transforming what is fundamentally a decolonization problem into an East-West issue. The Bureau therefore reiterates the categorical rejection of the linkage of the Namibian independence to the withdrawal of Cuban troops from Angola; it considers such linkage as repugnant to the United Nations Plan and a blatant interference in the internal affairs of the People's Republic of Angola and designed to subvert its sovereign rights as an independent state. The Bureau recalls that the Security Council, in Resolution 539 (1983), rejected that linkage.[78]

In the plan of action, the Bureau was quite specific in its recommendations:

Pending the imposition of mandatory sanctions against South Africa under Charter VII of the United Nations Charter, member states of the United Nations, in particular, members of the Non-Aligned Movement that have not done so, are exhorted to take voluntary measures to sever all links and dealings with South Africa, in accordance with United Nations General Assembly resolutions to that effect. Such measures should include:

   (i)   severance of diplomatic relations;

  (ii)   the observance of an oil embargo;

 (iii)   disinvestment of existing interests, prohibition of new investments and application of disincentives to this end;

 (iv)   the withholding of overflight and landing facilities to aircraft and docking rights to ocean vessels;

  (v)   the prohibition of the sale of Krugerrands and all other coins minted in South·Africa;

 (vi)   the strict observance of the sports and cultural boycott of South Africa; and

(vii)   the ratification and implementation of the International Convention on the Suppression and Punishment of the Crime of *Apartheid*.[79]

Thus the foreign ministers concluded in New Delhi that after having observed the failure of the Contact Group initiative and the U.S. policy of "constructive engagement" with South Africa, there was a need for the global community to bring new pressures upon the government of South Africa and to construct a new policy to bring about the independence of Namibia. It is for this reason that they demanded an urgent meeting of the UN Security Council.

6: Namibia and the United Nations Security Council

The UN Security Council met in June 1985 to take up the Namibian question. As is customary, non-aligned countries led by the African group held extensive discussions during the New Delhi meeting to determine their strategy at the SC meeting. From past experiences given the political composition of the Security Council, there are three different strategies that could be adopted on SC resolutions relating to apartheid and Namibia. The basic objective is to obtain a majority consensus on a resolution. However, the primary concern is whether the U.S. will exercise its veto on a given resolution, thus declaring its open support for the South African government and its policies.

In preparing the draft resolution for the Security Council, non-aligned and African countries have traditionally had three options, each with merits and drawbacks. The first is to produce a draft that is sufficiently vague and general which may not have immediate policy implications and, hence, becomes acceptable to the Contact Group and the United States. There are those within the non-aligned and African group which argue that a general resolution, however weak, would have its advantages, especially if the United States supports it. Such a resolution would certainly draw a consensus and, therefore, would send a distinct message to the South African government. On the other hand, the message may be so weak that the South African government could easily ignore it. The second option is to develop a compromise resolution, between what the Contact Group and what the non-aligned and African group would find acceptable. Such a compromise is normally brokered by a Western veto power other than the U.S. These Western veto powers, i.e., France and Great Britain, would then lobby the United States not to exercise the veto, but to abstain. Again, there are those within the non-aligned and African group which would argue that it is better to have the U.S. abstain than to veto. An abstention means a polite no, but the act of politeness would be communicated to the Republic of South Africa. The final option calls for a tough resolution, in this case, the applying of compulsory sanctions against South Africa. Such a resolution would be guaranteed to be vetoed by the United States, joined possibly by the other two Western veto powers. Here again there are those countries in the NAM and Africa which feel that such a strategy is absolutely essential in order to expose the linkage between the Western Contact Group and the Republic of South Africa. They argue that the Western countries should not be given an escape valve on the question and should be condemned for their actions internationally. The primary goal, nonetheless, is to bring sufficient pressure on the South African government to ensure its compliance with specific UN resolutions.

After having considered all these strategic options, a group of non-aligned countries, Burkina Faso, Egypt, India, Madagascar, Peru, and Trinidad and Tobago presented a draft resolution 566 to the Security Council which was considered by all to be reasonably strong. It included the items agreed to in the New Delhi Declaration and called for specific actions which would embarrass South Africa. The items that caused considerable debate related to the imposition of mandatory economic sanctions as well as certain voluntary sanctions against South Africa in an effort to bring it into compliance with UN resolutions. They were presented in the draft resolution to the Security Council as paragraphs 13 and 14 as follows:

The Security Council,.....

13. *Strongly warns* South Africa that failure to do so would compel the

Security Council to meet forthwith to impose, as a first step, mandatory economic sanctions against it under Chapter VII of the United Nations Charter as necessary additional pressure to ensure South Africa's compliance with the aforementioned resolutions;

14. *Urges* that pending the imposition of mandatory sanctions against South Africa under Chapter VII of the United Nations Charter Member States of the United Nations that have not done so take appropriate voluntary measures to sever all links and dealings with South Africa, which could include:

(a) Severance of diplomatic relations;
(b) The observance of an oil embargo;
(c) Disinvestment of existing interests, prohibition of new investments and application of disincentives to this end;
(d) The withholding of overflight and landing facilities to aircraft and docking rights to ocean vessels;
(e) The prohibition of the sale of krugerrands and all other coins minted in South Africa;
(f) The strict observance of the sports and cultural boycott of South Africa; and
(g) The ratification and implementation of the international convention on the suppression and punishment of the crime of *apartheid*.[80]

During the consultations of the draft resolution, it was evident that these particular items were totally unacceptable to the United States and the United Kingdom, and that France also had considerable misgivings. However, this resolution had the firm support of the entire third world and socialist world.

While various ministers and heads of delegations were making their speeches in support of Namibian independence, the Chair of the Council, at this time, Trinidad and Tobago, held extensive discussions with all delegations to formulate a compromise so that the resolution could be adopted without a veto. As the debate continued, SWAPO and the African group were convinced that they should keep up the strong pressure for the imposition of sanctions. They concluded that they could compromise on the issue of the compulsory sanctions, but there was to be no compromise on voluntary sanctions. In addition, the African group led by SWAPO was fully aware that while this resolution might fail, it was necessary to maintain constant international pressure for the implementation of economic sanctions with the view that the United States and other Western countries would eventually comply.

A liberation movement, like SWAPO, is forced to adopt a very delicate strategy in dealing with both its opponents and its friends during UN debates. It must exploit existing contradictions within the Western grouping, which has traditionally supported South Africa, to hopefully gain their support and, at the least, to minimize their opposition. In addition, it must be certain not to alienate the moderate countries of Europe and·Latin America which are also looking for a convenient way òut of the dilemma. Most importantly, it must not betray its strongest and most militant allies by softening the resolution. Taking all these factors into consideration, SWAPO sought a resolution that would provide the maximum benefit in pushing its case for independence forward. SWAPO's position was generally accepted by the non-aligned countries including the African group, as well as the socialist world and China.

The debate that ensued in the Security Council was influenced by a number of external events. Scarcely one month earlier, Angola announced that on May 24, 1985, it had captured South African commandoes inside its northern region as they were attempting to destroy U.S. owned oil installations. This South African military incursion deep inside Angolan territory had occurred after South Africa, with the brokering of the U.S., had adopted non-aggression pacts with Angola and Mozambique. There was then general opposition to this Cabinda incident. In addition, delegations were alarmed by South Africa's act of defiance in announcing on June 17 just prior to the Security Council meeting that it was installing an "interim government" in Namibia which was clearly contrary to UN resolutions. Others more accurately labelled it a puppet government and the issue caused a great deal of embarrassment, especially for the advocates of "constructive engagement." Consequently, they were forced to disassociate themselves from the action and condemn it. The United States delegate, Mr. Sorzano, quoted his government's position on South Africa's "interim government."

It has long been our position, and that of our Contact Group partners, that any purported transfer of power that might take place now or in the future to bodies established in Namibia by South Africa is null and void. Such institutions will have, as Secretary Schultz stated on April 16, no standing. We have not recognized them in the past and will not do so now. Our negotiating effort continues with the governments concerned. Thus, we view the announcement regarding internal administrative arrangements inside Namibia as without effect on these negotiations or the agreements already achieved thereunder.[82]

He also indicated that the U.S. was opposed to South Africa's "cross-border violence" and in reference to Pretoria's activities in Cabinda he stated:

... Respect for the national sovereignty of all states and the inviolability of international borders is a key principle in international relations. The United States cannot condone violations of this principle in whatever direction they may be launched or in the name of whatever goal they may be justified. In this regard, we deplore South African violations of Angolan territorial integrity. Violent actions across borders, be they military attacks, sabotage or terrorism against innocent civilians, can only serve to undermine the confidence necessary for the settlement of disputes. In this instance, they can only detract from the prospects of the early independence of Namibia.[83]

The question of Cuban troops in Angola as a precondition to negotiations was raised in the discussions again by a number of Western states. The Cuban Minister was quick to respond once more that the independence of Namibia was unrelated to the issue of Cuban troops. As far as Cuba and the NAM was concerned there could be no compromise on the question. Cuban troops had been invited by Angola and were regarded as necessary to defend Angola from South Africa's attacks. He firmly supported this position by quoting President Fidel Castro's remarks to Namibian students made in the presence of the secretary general of the United Nations.

"There will be no solution in southern Africa without resolution 435 (1978) and without the independence of Namibia. And Angola is so much in agreement with this - and I do not doubt in the slightest that this is Angola's position - that so long as resolution 435 (1978) is not implemented and so long as Namibia is not independent, or at least while all the concrete, necessary steps are not being taken for the implementation of the resolution and the genuine, effective attainment of its independence, not a single Cuban soldier will be withdrawn from Angola. If there is a need for more soldiers, we shall send more, because when confronted with each act of aggression by imperialism and racists, we have always reacted by strengthening Angola."[84]

South Africa's response has been to increase its military activities in the region. Besides its Angola raid, South Africa also sent forces into Botswana claiming it was acting in self-defence and killed civilians. Both Botswana and Angola immediately called for an emergency meeting of the Security Council after the Namibia debate to discuss these blatant violations.

These two issues led a number of moderate and conservative countries to actively participate in the Security Council debate. Nearly 70 countries and organizations asked to speak and called for a strong condemnation of South Africa. In spite of this massive global solidarity, which included the countries of Africa, the non-aligned world, the European countries, the socialist world, and indeed the United States, the South African delegate did not take their arguments seriously. In his response, he repeated the traditional South African view that the only issue in the way of Namibian independence is the presence of Cuban troops.[85] He also defended his government's "interim mechanism for the internal administration" of Namibia and its military action in Angola. In his explanation, however, he placed the blame on the United Nations and the Security Council and held them responsible because of their support for national liberation. The South African delegate stated:

In the circumstances, the South African security forces have felt it necessary to gather intelligence on the activities of the ANC and SWAPO terrorists in Angola and to consider appropriate counter-actions. . . .

There should, however, be no doubt about the root cause of what happened in Cabinda. It was the Angolan Government's blatant disregard of international law in allowing and encouraging the ANC to train and to prepare for acts of violence against South Africa. The Angolan Government is, however, not the only culprit. *This Organization and many members of this Council must share the responsibility for having actively encouraged and supported the terrorist activities of the ANC and SWAPO.*[86] (emphasis ours)

Finally, as an admonition to the Western countries, the South African delegate raised questions about their political judgments, including their values, and made a most amazing proposal for consideration by the Council:

> The time has come for Western countries in this Organization to take a stand for the promotion of the democratic values which they profess to espouse. We challenge them to commission some impartial and reputable organization such as Freedom House to carry out an objective and comparative study of the state of human, political, economic and civil rights in all the countries of the world. Such a study should judge whether Governments are attempting to increase possibilities for participation in the political process or to restrict such developments. It should also provide an analysis of the constitutions, record, associations and actions of movements such as SWAPO and the ANC. South Africa would be prepared to co-operate fully with any such study.[87]

The South African interventions during the debate proved far too embarrassing for the Security Council to take these pronouncements seriously. The procedure that evolved in arriving at a final resolution followed a well established script at the Security Council. A compromise solution was presented by France in the last stages of the debate that omitted mandatory sanctions and retained voluntary sanctions with the provision that the Security Council would take further action if South Africa did not comply with certain actions. This was in conformity with the minimum that SWAPO and the NAM would accept.

France has always been placed in an awkward situation on the question of sanctions and the isolation of South Africa. While the French have extensive trade relations with South Africa, they are also not anxious to alienate their allies in Francophone Africa, nor their trading partners in the entire third world. In addition, France is presently led by a socialist government which has tried on various occasions to distance itself from the conservative coalition of its Western counterparts—the United Kingdom, West Germany, and the United States. The United Kingdom, on the other hand, remained in agreement with the United States on the question of sanctions. However, the U.K. was also anxious to retain its links, especially trade links with Asian, African, and Caribbean members of the Commonwealth and, hence, was also pleased with a compromise. While it was obvious to non-aligned and African members that the United States would most likely abstain on this resolution, they saw an abstention as a clear victory and argued for the compromise.

It is for these reasons that after considerable last minute discussions, items 13 and 14 in the original draft were changed with the following wording:

The Security Council,. . . .

13. *Strongly warns* South Africa that failure to do so would compel the Security Council to meet forthwith to consider the adoption of additional measures under the United Nations Charter, including Chapter VII, as additional pressure to ensure South Africa's compliance with the above-mentioned resolutions.

14. *Urges* Member States of the United Nations that have not done so to consider in the meantime taking appropriate voluntary measures against South Africa, which could include:

1) stopping of new investments and application of disincentives to this end;
2) re-examination of maritime and aerial relations with South Africa;
3) the prohibition of the sale of krugerrands and all other coins minted in South Africa;
4) restrictions in the field of sports and cultural relations.[88]

With this compromise on mandatory sanctions, but the inclusion of voluntary sanctions, Security Council resolution 566 was adopted 13 in favor, none against, and with 2 abstentions. In spite of this compromise, the United States and the United Kingdom still chose to abstain. The United States explained its abstention with the following:

Our desire to make clear our opposition to South Africa's action in Namibia has convinced us not to oppose this resolution. However, there were a number of elements in it on which we are not in agreement and which led us, reluctantly, to abstain. We find it hard to reaffirm resolutions that we did not affirm in the first place. Our central concern is that *mandatory* sanctions are not likely to advance the cause of peace and Namibian independence. Rather, it is our judgment that they are likely to retard that goal. We also believe that economic development is likely to encourage the necessary social and political changes in South Africa and promote the elimination of the abhorrent policy of *apartheid*. We cannot, therefore, in good faith conscientiously join in urging others to undertake actions which we believe would slow down the achievement of that objective.[89]

On the other hand, those who argued for a stronger statement on sanctions in the resolution, such as the socialist countries as well as China and a number of non-aligned countries agreed to accept the majority consensus on the issue. In their view, the resolution was a victory, there was no veto. The global community, including the United States and the Western Contact Group members, had sent a clear signal to the Government of South Africa that support for its policies had seriously eroded and that there was international support for the implementation of UN resolutions in support of the independence of Namibia.

As the debate came to a close, President Nujoma of SWAPO took the floor to thank the friends of the Namibian people and to admonish their enemies. At the same time, he had some sharp words for those who sat on the fence and reminded them of the implications of their position:

> The notorious policy of constructive engagement, together with its hated offshoot, the pre-condition of linkage, was roundly condemned, and the collusion of its authors, Washington and Pretoria, thoroughly exposed. These pernicious and racist policies stand firmly rejected by all because their objective is to entrench *apartheid* further, to delay the independence of Namibia, and to weaken the independent African States in the region, in an effort to make them dependent on *apartheid* South Africa. The primary interest of the United States of America, in collaboration with the Afrikaner regime, is to perpetuate the *status quo*, namely the continued, unfettered plunder of natural resources by the transnational corporations, and the enslavement of the African majority in South Africa and Namibia.[90]

RESOLUTION 566 (1985)
Adopted by the Security Council at its 2595th meeting, on 19 June 1985

The Security Council,

Having considered the reports of the Secretary-General (S/16237 and S/17242),

Having heard the statement by the Acting President of the United Nations Council for Namibia,

Having considered the statement by Dr. Sam Nujoma, President of the South West Africa People's Organization (SWAPO)

Commending the South West Africa People's Organization for its preparedness to co-operate fully with the United Nations Secretary-General and his Special Representative, including its expressed readiness to sign and observe a cease-fire agreement with South Africa, in the implementation of the United Nations Plan for Namibia as embodied in Security Council resolution 435 (1978),

Recalling General Assembly resolutions 1514 (XV) of 14 December 1960 and 2145 (XXI) of 27 October 1966,

Recalling and reaffirming its resolutions 269 (1969), 276 (1970), 301 (1971), 385 (1976), 431 (1978), 432 (1978), 435 (1978), 439 (1978), 532 (1983) and 539 (1983),

Recalling the statement of the President of the Security Council (S/17151) of 3 May 1985, on behalf of the Council, which, *inter alia*, declared the establishment of the so-called interim government in Namibia to be null and void,

Gravely concerned at the tension and instability created by the hostile policies of the *apartheid* régime throughout southern Africa and the mounting threat to the security of the region and its wider implications for international peace and security resulting from that régime's continued utilization of Namibia as a springboard for military attacks against and destabilization of African States in the region,

Reaffirming the legal responsibility of the United Nations over Namibia and the primary responsibility of the Security Council for ensuring the implementation of its resolutions, in particular resolutions 385 (1976) and 435 (1978) which contain the United Nations Plan for Namibian independence,

Noting that 1985 marks the fortieth anniversary of the founding of the United Nations, as well as the twenty-fifth anniversary of the adoption of the Declaration on the Granting of Independence to Colonial Countries and Peoples, and expressing grave concern that the question of Namibia has been with the Organization since its inception and still remains unresolved,

Welcoming the emerging and intensified world-wide campaign of people from all spheres of life against the racist régime of South Africa in a concerted effort to bring about an end to the illegal occupation of Namibia and of *apartheid*,

1. *Condemns* South Africa for its continued illegal occupation of Namibia in flagrant defiance of resolutions of the General Assembly and decisions of the Security Council of the United Nations;

2. *Reaffirms* the legitimacy of the struggle of the Namibian people against the illegal occupation of the racist régime of South Africa and calls upon all States to increase their moral and material assistance to them;

3. *Further condemns* the racist régime of South Africa for its installation of a so-called interim government in Windhoek and declares that this action, taken even while the Security Council has been in session, constitutes a direct affront to it and a clear defiance of its resolutions, particularly resolutions 435 (1978) and 439 (1978);

4. *Declares* that action to be illegal and null and void and states that no recognition will be accorded either by the United Nations or any Member State to it or to any representative or organ established in pursuance thereof;

5. *Demands* that the racist régime of South Africa immediately rescind the aforementioned illegal and unilateral action;

6. *Further condemns* South Africa for its obstruction of the implementation of Security Council resolution 435 (1978) by insisting on conditions contrary to the provisions of the United Nations Plan for the independence of Namibia;

7. *Rejects once again* South Africa's insistence on linking the independence of Namibia to irrelevant and extraneous issues as incompatible with resolution 435 (1978), other decisions of the Security Council and the resolutions of the General Assembly of Namibia, including General Assembly resolution 1514 (XV) of 14 December 1960;

8. *Declares once again* that the independence of Namibia cannot be held hostage to the resolution of issues that are alien to Security Council resolution 435 (1978);

9. *Reiterates* that Security Council resolution 435 (1978), embodying the United Nations Plan for the independence of Namibia, is the only internationally accepted basis for a peaceful settlement of the Namibian problem and demands its immediate and unconditional implementation;

10. *Affirms* that the consultations undertaken by the Secretary-General pursuant to paragraph 5 of resolution 532 (1983) have confirmed

that all the outstanding issues relevant to Security Council resolution 435 (1978) have been resolved, except for the choice of the electoral system;

11. *Decides* to mandate the Secretary-General to resume immediate contact with South Africa with a view to obtaining its choice of the electoral system to be used for the election, under United Nations supervision and control, for the Constituent Assembly, in terms of resolution 435 (1978), in order to pave the way for the adoption by the Security Council of the enabling resolution for implementation of the United Nations Independence Plan for Namibia;

12. *Demands* that South Africa co-operate fully with the Security Council and the Secretary-General in the implementation of the present resolution;

13. *Strongly warns* South Africa that failure to do so would compel the Security Council to meet forthwith to consider the adoption of appropriate measures under the United Nations Charter, including Chapter VII, as additional pressure to ensure South Africa's compliance with the above-mentioned resolutions;

14. *Urges* Member States of the United Nations that have not done so to consider in the meantime taking appropriate voluntary measures against South Africa, which could include

(a)   Stopping of new investments and application of disincentives to this end;

(b)   Re-examination of maritime and aerial relations with South Africa;

(c)   The prohibition of the sale of krugerrands and all other coins minted in South Africa;

(d)   Restrictions in the field of sports and cultural relations;

15. *Requests* the Secretary-General to report on the implementation of the present resolution not later than the first week of September 1985;

16. *Decides* to remain seized of the matter and to meet immediately upon receipt of the Secretary-General's report for the purpose of reviewing progress in the implementation of resolution 435 (1978) and, in the event of continued obstruction by South Africa, to invoke paragraph 13 above.

Conclusions

The Republic of South Africa has put into motion a well orchestrated global design to put the Namibian question into a permanent cul-de-sac. The linkage doctrine has been fine tuned and new promises and conditions are constantly being introduced to confuse the negotiations process. Under these circumstances, it is obvious that South Africa is determined to impose a military solution. However, it received a serious setback during its last military intervention into southern Angola. Angola revealed that it could handle the air war against South Africa and successfully stopped the ground attack. Not only were Cuban troops not involved in this fighting as even U.S. business and intelligence sources noted, but Angola is clearly proving to be militarily self-sufficient.[91]

The Republic of South Africa continues, however, to challenge the security and sovereignty of Angola, the front line states, and indeed all of Africa. The Cabinda incident of May 1985, which took place after South Africa had announced with great fanfare that it was withdrawing its troops from Angola in keeping with the government's new non-aggression pacts with Angola and Mozambique, and the Botswana attack on civilians of June 1985 reveals that the Republic of South Africa is determined to pursue a military solution. It has adopted three methods: first, the use of conventional troops for invasions; second, the use of "contras," like Savimbi, to destabilize and delegitimize governments; and third, clandestine commandoes to disrupt the economy.

The NAM has begun to re-examine the nature of its support for national liberation movements, especially its military and security policy in the southern Africa region and globally. Non-aligned countries have developed considerable military expertise during their struggle for independence and after independence to protect their national sovereignty. India and Nigeria, for example, have well disciplined standing armies. Algeria and Vietnam have established the fact that by adopting guerrilla strategies they were able to defeat France and the U.S. There is, in addition, the wealth of the Middle East whose countries have been able to purchase the most advanced modern technological systems. Thus the non-aligned may have to explore the possibility of utilizing these enormous resources to protect the sovereignty of its members in southern Africa and especially to maintain peace in the region.

Non-aligned countries have consistently entrusted the United Nations with multilateral diplomacy and international decision-making. With the efforts of the non-aligned countries, the General Assembly has supported the rights of the Namibian people to self-determination and independence and SWAPO as their sole authentic representative. The problem now lies within the Security Council and specifically with the Western veto power members.

The NAM has also relied on the UN to undertake peace-keeping functions, but the recent massive attack on the UN system by the West is slowly eroding the effectiveness of that institution, whether it be in the area of education, such as UNESCO, or the economy, UNCTAD. If these attacks on the multilateral efforts of the UN continue, non-aligned countries will have to find other ways to maintain its principles and to protect the integrity and sovereignty of its members. In addition, the movement presently faces the fundamental question of how to protect its members in southern Africa from the military attacks of South Africa. In the 1940's, all of Europe joined forces to deal with fascist Germany. The global community is faced with a similar phenomenon in southern Africa. The NAM has called attention to the crisis in southern Africa and its consequences for Namibia and the world at large. It has provided international support and solidarity for the people of Namibia and SWAPO in spite of the efforts of South Africa and its allies to discredit the activities of the movement. The time may be approaching when non-aligned countries will have to lead a global movement to deal with this 21st century "bully" in southern Africa which is holding not only Namibia, but the entire world hostage with its nuclear capability, in order to fulfill its national interests which are in violation of the UN Charter.

It has become customary of cynics, both in the West and within the NAM, to dismiss non-aligned declarations as pious homilies. It would be useful if these cynics paid heed to the President of SWAPO, Sam Nujoma, whose people have been victims of terror and degradation for over one hundred years and have yet to see Namibia's "sacred trust" within the international community fulfilled. President Nujoma told the closing session of the New Delhi Extraordinary Meeting of non-aligned countries that the Final Declaration "has reinforced our belief that most of the non-aligned countries are behind our cause" and that the people of Namibia would view it as a profound source of inspiration.

Today the world is faced with the obscenity of an illegitimate regime in the southern half of the African continent which has plundered the resources of the African people and used these resources to conduct a war of genocide against the peoples of southern Africa, while to the north another region, again a victim of European exploitation, is experiencing famine, death, and malnutrition. History will never forgive the global community if it sits idly by and watches this process without making real efforts to reverse these trends and create the conditions for social, economic, and political justice on the African continent.

Notes

1. This section is drawn from Chapter 9, of our forthcoming book-length manuscript, entitled "Non-Alignment in an Age of Alignments" and is an expanded and revised version of Chapter III of A.W. Singham and S. Hune, *The Non-Aligned Movement and the Namibian Question* (Chandigarh, India: Centre for Research in Rural and Industrial Development, 1985), pp. 14–33.
2. "Update on Namibia: Is There Cause for Optimism," *TransAfrica Forum Issue Brief* 1:8 (Washington, D.C.: September 1982).
3. O. Jankowitsch and Karl Sauvant. *The Third World Without Superpowers: The Collected Documents of the Non-Aligned Countries* (Dobbs Ferry, NY: Oceana Publications, 1978), I, p. 3.
4. Ibid., p. 46.
5. *Two Decades of Non-Alignment: Documents of the Gatherings of the Non-Aligned Countries 1961–1982* (New Delhi, India: Ministery of External Affairs, Government of India, 1983), item 5, p. 19.
6. Geisa Maria Rocha. *In Search of Namibian Independence* (Boulder and London: Westview Press, 1984), pp. 53–5, 68–73.
7. *Two Decades of Non-Alignment*, pp. 53–4.
8. Rocha, pp. 86–7.
9. *Two Decades of Non-Alignment*, pp. 131–32.
10. Ibid., item 34, p. 144.
11. Ibid., especially items 6 and 10, pp. 180–81.
12. Study Commission on U.S. Policy Toward Southern Africa. *South Africa: Time Running Out* (Berkeley: University of California Press, 1981), pp. 353–4.
13. *Two Decades of Non-Alignment*, item 21, p. 191.
14. Ibid., pp. 224–25.
15. Ibid., pp. 277–79.
16. Ibid., item 21, p. 298.
17. Ibid., items 12 and 13, p. 339.
18. Ibid., p. 356.
19. Ibid., item 7, p. 360.
20. Ibid., item 3, p. 360.
21. Ibid., items 20 and 21, pp. 361–62.

22. Ibid., items 51–4, pp. 364–65.
23. Ibid., items 30–35, pp. 372–73.
24. Ibid., item 24, p. 405.
25. Ibid., items 65 and 66, p. 409.
26. Ibid., items 40–49, p. 503.
27. Final Communique of the Front Line States Summit Meeting, Luanda, April 15, 1981. Doc/12.
28. Sam Nujoma, Address by the President of SWAPO before the Extraordinary Ministerial Meeting of the Non-Aligned Countries Co-Ordination Bureau of Namibia, Algiers, 18 April 1981.
29. *Two Decades of Non-Alignment: Documents of the Gatherings of the Non-Aligned Countries 1961–1982* (New Delhi, India: Ministry of External Affairs, Government of India, 1983), pp. 535–40.
30. Ibid., pp. 541–44.
31. Ibid., items 24–27, p. 597.
32. *Final Documents* Seventh Conference of Heads of State or Government, New Delhi, March 1983, p. 17–18.
33. Ibid., p. 194.
34. Ibid., pp. 15, 201.
35. *South Africa: Time Running Out*, pp. 356–65.
36. Chester Crocker, "South Africa: Strategy for Change," *Foreign Affairs* (Winter 1980/81).
37. Chester Crocker, Honolulu Speech, August 29, 1981.
38. Report of the International Conference in Support of the Struggle of the Namibian People for Independence, Paris, 25–29 April 1983 (New York: United Nations, 1983), A/CONF.120/13, p. 83.
39. Ibid., p. 84.
40. Ibid., pp. 8–9.
41. Ibid., p. 60.
42. Ibid.
43. Abdul S. Minty, "Namibia: A Review of Developments since the 1980 International Conference in Solidarity with the Struggle of the People of Namibia," prepared for the International Conference in Support of the Struggle of the Namibian People for Independence, Paris, 25–29 April 1983.
44. Report of the United Nations Council for Namibia, "Activities of Foreign Economic Interests Operating in Namibia," (New York: United Nations), A/CONF.120/4 A/AC.131/92, 16 March 1983, p. 7.
45. Report of the United Nations Council for Namibia, "Social Conditions in Namibia," (New York: United Nations), A/CONF.120/5 A/AC.131/93, 16 March 1983, p. 12.
46. Report of the United Nations Council for Namibia, "The Military Situation in and Relating to Namibia," (New York: United Nations), A/CONF.120/3 A/AC.131/91, 28 March 1983, p. 11.
47. Mr. Sam Nujoma, United Nations Security Council, S/PV.2439, 23 May 1983, p. 71.
48. Mr. von Schirnding, United Nations Security Council, S/PV.2481, 20 October 1983, p. 27.
49. Ibid., p. 31.
50. Mr. Lichenstein, United Nations Security Council, S/PV.2450, 31 May 1983, p. 28.
51. Mr. Nujoma, Ibid., pp. 20–21.
52. Further Report of the Secretary-General Concerning the Implementation of Security Council Resolutions 435 (1978) and 439 (1978) Concerning the Question of Namibia, (New York: United Nations Security Council), S/15943, 29 August 1983, p. 4.

53. Mr. von Schirnding, United Nations Security Council, S/PV.2481, 20 October 1983.
54. Mr. Mueshihange, Ibid., pp. 62–3.
55. Mr. Pelletier, United Nations Security Council, S/PV.2488, 26 October 1983, p. 28.
56. Mr. van Well, United Nations Security Council, S/PV.2486, 25 October 1983, p. 17.
57. Sir John Thomson, United Nations Security Council, S/PV.2492, 28 October 1983, p. 26.
58. Mrs. Kirkpatrick, United Nations Security Council, S/PV.2484, 24 October 1983, p. 28.
59. Mr. Ramachandran, United Nations General Assembly, A/38/PV.74, 1 December 1983, pp. 5, 8–9.
60. Mr. von Schirnding, United Nations Security Council, S/PV.2504, 16 December 1983, pp. 11, 17–18.
61. Mrs. Kirkpatrick, United Nations Security Council, S/PV.2508, 20 December 1983, p. 18.
62. Mr. de Figueiredo, United Nations Security Council, S/PV.2504, 16 December 1983, p. 8.
63. Further report of the Secretary-General Concerning the Implementation of Security Council Resolutions 435 (1978) and 439 (1978) concerning the Question of Namibia, United Nations Security Council, S/16237, 29 December 1983, p. 4.
64. This section has been drawn in part from A.W. Singham, "Namibia: Politics of Postponement" *Mainstream* (India) (December 8, 1984), pp. 9–10, 34.
65. Jonathan Friedland, "Angola: Will U.S. 'linkage' policy backfire?" *The City Sun* (New York) (Feb. 27–March 5, 1985), p. 8.
66. Ibid.
67. Ibid.
68. Ibid.
69. We are grateful to Gay McDougall for her testimony presented to the Hearings on Namibia before the Subcommittee on Africa of the Committee on Foreign Affairs of the U.S. House of Representatives at the 99th Congress, 1st session, February 21, 1985.
70. For details on the legal and constitutional aspects, see Part III of our forthcoming book, "Non-Alignment in an Age of Alignments."
71. Department of Information and Publicity, SWAPO of Namibia. *To Be Born a Nation: The Liberation Struggle for Namibia* (London: Zed Press, 1981), p. 293.
72. Ibid.
73. Extraordinary Ministerial Meeting of the Co-ordinating Bureau of Non-Aligned Countries on the Question of Namibia,"Inaugural Address by H.E. Shri Rajiv Gandhi Prime Minister of India," (New Delhi, April 1985), NAC/CONF. 7/NCB (S-I)/Doc. 6, 19 April 1985, p. 3.
74. Extraordinary Ministerial Meeting of the Co-ordinating Bureau of Non-Aligned Countries on the Question of Namibia, "Draft Statement Condemning South Africa's Decision to Install a So-Called 'Internal Administration' in Namibia," (New Delhi, April 1985), NAC/CONF. 7/NCB (S-I)/Doc. 8, 19 April 1985, p. 1.
75. Extraordinary Ministerial Meeting, "Inaugural Address by H.E. Shri Rajiv Gandhi," p. 2.
76. Extraordinary Ministerial Meeting of the Co-ordinating Bureau of Non-Aligned Countries on the Question of Namibia, "Draft Final Document," (New Delhi, 19–21 April 1985), NAC/CONF. 7/NCB (S-I)/Doc. 1/Rev. 1, 21 April 1985, items 38 and 39, p. 8.
77. Ibid., item 30, p. 7.
78. Ibid., item 25, p. 6.
79. Ibid., item 55, p. 11.

80. United Nations, Security Council, *Burkina Faso, Egypt, India, Madagascar, Peru and Trinidad and Tobago: draft resolution*, S/17284, 18 June 1985, p. 3.

81. "South Africa Admits Spy Mission After Angola Accuses It of a Raid," *New York Times* (May 24, 1985) and "U.S. Seeking Explanation," *New York Times* (May 25, 1985).

82. United States Mission to the United Nations, *Press Release*, USUN 58–(85), June 12, 1985, p. 2.

83. Ibid., p. 3.

84. United Nations, Security Council, *Provisional Verbatim Record of the Two Thousand Five Hundred and Eighty-Fourth Meeting*, S/PV.2584, 11 June 1985, p. 24.

85. United Nations, Security Council, *Provisional Verbatim Record of the Two Thousand Five Hundred and Eighty-Third Meeting*, S/PV.2583, 10 June 1985, p. 96.

86. Ibid., p. 102.

87. Ibid., pp. 99–100.

88. United Nations, Security Council, *Press Release* SC/4713, 19 June 1985.

89. United Nations, Security Council, *Provisional Verbatim Record of the Two Thousand Five Hundred and Ninety-Fifth Meeting*, S/PV.2595, 19 June 1985, p. 18.

90. United Nations, Security Council, *Provisional Verbatim Record of the Two Thousand Five Hundred and Ninety-Meetings*, S/PV.2595, 19 June 1985, p. 18.

91. David Martin and Phyllis Johnson, "Africa: The Old and the Unexpected" *Foreign Affairs* 63:3 (1985), p. 611.

Select Bibliography on Namibia

Books

Afrikaanse Handelsinstituut. Streek Suidwes-Afrika. *This is South West Africa.* Windhoek: Afrikaanse Handelsinstituut-Streek Suidwes-Afrika, 1976. 80 p.

Adams, Samuel C., Jr. *Zimbabwe, Namibia: Anticipation of Economic and Humanitarian Needs; Transition Problems of Developing Nations in Southern Africa; Final Report.* Washington: African-American Scholars Council, 1977. 388 p.

Adelman, Kenneth L., and Seiler, John. *Alternative Futures in Southern Africa.* Arlington, Va.: SRI International, Strategic Studies Center, 1979. 107 p.

Amnesty International. *Namibia: Amnesty International Briefing.* London: Amnesty International Publications, 1977. 16 p.

Apartheid's Army in Namibia: South Africa's Illegal Military Occupation. London: International Defence and Aid Fund, 1982. 74 p.

Asian African Legal Consultative Committee. *South West Africa Cases; Report of the Committee and Background Materials.* New Delhi, Secretariat of the Committee, 1968. 414 p.

Babing, Alfred. *Namibia: Kolonialzeit, Widerstand, Befreiungskampf heute.* Cologne: Pahl-Rugenstein, 1980. 221 p.

Baker, Donald G. *Zimbabwe and Namibia: Final Report.* Washington: African-American Scholars Council, 1977. 61, 28, 31 leaves.

Barratt, John, et al. *The Future of South West Africa/Namibia: A Symposium.* Braamfontein: South Africa Institute of International Affairs, 1977. 14 p.

Booh, Jacques-Roger. *La Decolonisation de la Namibie: un mandat usurpé.* Paris: Les Publications universitaires, c1982. 295 p.

Botha, R. F. *Aanklag en verweer in die Suidwes-Afrika-saak voor die wereldhof.* Potchefstroom: Sentrum vir Internasionale Politiek, Potchefstroomse Universiteit vir Christelike Hoer Onderwys, 1974. 63 p.

———. *South West Africa and the United Nations: South African Letter Addressed to the U.N. Secretary-General on 27 January 1976.* Johannesburg: South African Institute of International Affairs, 1976. 18 p.

———. *SWAPO: Dialogue or Conflict?* Sandton, South Africa: Southern African Freedom Foundation, 1977. 30 p.

Brandt, Hartmut, et al. *Perspectives of Independent Development in Southern Africa: The Cases of Zimbabwe and Namibia.* Translated by Douglas Ross. Berlin: German Development Institute, 1980. xiv, 183 p.

Braum, Robert Love, ed. *Southwest Africa Under Mandate: Documents on the Administration of the Former German Protectorate of Southwest Africa by the Union of South Africa under Mandate of the League of Nations, 1919–1929.* Salisbury, N.C.: Documentary Publications, 1976. v, 241 p.

Bridgman, Jon. *The Revolt of the Hereros.* Berkeley: University of California Press, 1981. 184 p.

British Council of Churches. Division of International Affairs. *Namibia.* London: The Council, 198. (4) 23 p.

Bruckner de Villiers Research. *A Bruckner de Villiers Report on Recent Political and Constitutional Developments in South West Africa: A Survey of the Namibian Impasse.* Johannesburg: Bruckner de Villiers Research (Southern Africa), 1976. 46 p.

Bruwer, J. P. van S. *Ons mandaat Suidwes Afrika.* Johannesburg: SAUK, 1961. 27 p.

Burchfield, Susan, et al. *Black Women Under Apartheid: Our Sisters in Southern Africa.* Minneapolis, MN: Augsburg Publishing House, 1982. 31 p.

Carroll, Faye. *South West Africa and the United Nations.* Westport, Conn.: Greenwood Press, 1975. vii, 123 p.

Cilliers, Andries Charl. *The South West African Mandate in United Nations Context.* Pretoria: Institute of Foreign and Comparative Law, University of South Africa, 1976. x, 314 p.

Cockram, Gail-Maryse. *South West African Mandate.* Cape Town: Juta, 1976. 531 p.

Colligan, Paddy. *Soweto Remembered: Conversations With Freedom Fighters.* Atlanta: World View Publishers, 1981. xvi, 115 p.

Conference internationale de Dakar sur la Namibie et les droits de l'homme, 1976. *La Namibie et les droits de l'homme: d'hier à demain.* Centre international d'échanges, 5–8 janvier 1976: sous la presidence de Keba M'Baye. Paris: A. Pedone, 1976. p. 210–569.

Cooper, Allan D. *U.S. Economic Power and Political Influence in Namibia, 1700–1982.* Boulder, Colo.: Westview Press, 1982. xx, 222 p.

Co-ordinating Bureau of Non-Aligned Countries. *Extraordinary Ministerial Meeting of the Co-ordinating Bureau of the Non-Aligned Countries, Maputo, 26 January–2 February 1979 Final Communiqué.* New York: United Nations Document (A/34/126), 1979. 19 p.

Crocker, Chester A., and Hartland-Thunberg, Penelope. *Namibia at the Crossroads: Economic and Political Prospects.* Washington Center for Strategic and International Studies, 1978. 55 p.

Cronje, Gilliam. *The Workers of Namibia*. London: International Defence and Aid Fund, 1979. 135 p.

Cuadra, Hector. *La polemica sobre el colonialismo en las aciones Unidas: el caso de Namibia*. Mexico: UNAM, Instituto de Investigaciones Juridicas, 1975. 138 p.

Decalo, Samuel. *South-West Africa, 1960–1968: An Introductory Bibliography*. Kingston, University of Rhode Island, 1968. 20 leaves.

Der Gegenwartige Stand der Wirtschaft in Sudwestafrika/Namibia/zusammengestellt vom Direktorat fur Finanzen. Windhoek: SWA/Namibia Informationsamt, 1980. 12 p.

Documentation on U.N. Pre-Implementaion Meeting on Namibia: Geneva, January 7–14, 1981. Geneva, Switzerland: Lutheran World Federation and World Council of Churches, 1981. vi, 234 p.

Dore, Isaak Ismail. *The International Mandate System and Namibia*. Boulder, Colo.: Westview Press, 1985.

Drechsler, Horst. *Let Us Die Fighting: The Struggle of the Herero and Nama Against German Imperialism (1884–1915)*. Translated by Bernd Zollner. London: Zed Press, 1980. x, 277 p.

Dugard, C. J. R. *"Namibia and Human Rights": A Report on the Dakar Conference and Its Implications for the South West Africa Issue and Detente*. Braamfontein: South African Institute of International Affairs, 1976. 19 p.

————. *South West Africa and the International Court: Two Viewpoints on the 1971 Advisory Opinion*. Johannesburg: South African Institute of International Affairs, 1973 or 1974. 31 p.

————. *The South West Africa/Namibia Dispute: Documents and Scholarly Writings on the Controversy Between South Africa and the United Nations*. Berkeley: University of California Press, 1973. xix, 585 p.

Duignan, Peter. *South West Africa—Namibia*. New York: American African Affairs Association, 1978, 37 p.

Du Pisani, Andre. *Namibia Since Geneva*. Braamfontein, S.A.: South African Institute of International Affairs, 1981. 21 p.

————. *A Review of the Diplomatic Efforts of the Western Contact Group on Namibia, 1976–1980*. Braamfontein, South Africa: South African Institute of International Affairs, 1980. 8 p.

————, ed. *South West Africa/Namibia: The South African Government's Response to the U.N. Secretary-General's Report on the Implementation of the Western Proposal: The Government's Statement of 20 September 1978 and an Analysis*. Braamfontein, South Africa: South African Institute of International Affairs, 1978. 9 p.

————. SWA/Namibie: *probleme en beleidskeuses verbonde aan politieke oorgang*. Braamfontein: SUid-Afrikaanse Instituut van Internasionale Aangeleenthede, 1979. ii 8, 4 p.

Ellis, Justin. *Education, Repression and Liberation: Namibia.* London: World University Service. Catholic Institute for International Relations, 1984. 94 p.

———. *Elections in Namibia?* London: British Council of Churches, Catholic Institute for International Relations, 1979. 63 p.

Eriksen, Tore Linne. *Namibia: kolonialisme, apartheid og frigj}ringskamp i det s}rlige Afrika.* Uppsala: Nordiska afrikainstitutet; Oslo: Universitetsforlaget, 1982. 251 p.

Ermacora, Felix. *Namibia: Sudwestafrika.* Munchen: Bayerische Landeszentrale fur Politische Bildungsarbeit, 1981. 187 p.

Fraenkel, Peter J. *The Namibians of South West Africa.* London: Minority Rights Group, 1974. 48 p.

Germani, Hans. *Rettet Sudwest: am Schicksal der ehemaligen deutschen Kolonie, dem heutigen Namibia, entscheidet sich die Zukunft Afrikas.* Munchen: Herbig, 1982. 187 p.

Ghana. *Information Paper, Prepared by the Government of Ghana in Relation to Apartheid Laws Applying in the Mandated Territory of South West Africa and the Union of South Africa.* Accra: The Government Printer, 1960. 14 p.

Goldsworthy, David. *The International Politics of the Namibia Dispute.* Canberra, Australia: Dept. of the Parliamentary Library, 1982. 41 p.

Gorbunov, IU. I. *Namibiia, problemy dostizheniia nezavisimosti.* Moscow: Izd-vo "Nauka," Glav. red. vostochnoij lit-ry, 1983. 123 p.

Gordon, Robert J. *Mines, Masters and Migrants: Life in a Namibian Mine Compound.* Johannesburg: Ravan Press, 1977. 276 p.

Green, Reginald Herbold. *From Sudwestafrika to Namibia: The Political Economy of Transition.* Uppsala: Scandinavian Institute of African Studies, 1981. 51 p.

———. *Namibia: A Political Economic Survey.* Brighton: Institute of Development Studies, University of Sussex, 1979. 123 p.

———, ed. *Namibia, the Last Colony.* Essex: Longman, 1981. ix, 310 p.

Gross, Ernest A., et al. *Ethiopia and Liberia Versus South Africa: The South West Africa Cases.* Los Angeles: African Studies Center, University of California, 1968. 41 p.

Gutteridge, William Frank. *South Africa, Strategy for Survival?* London: Institute for the Study of Conflict, 1981. 32 p.

Halbach, Axel J. *Entwicklungsprobleme im sudlichen Afrika.* Munchen: Ifo-Institut fur Wirtschaftschung: Weltforum, 1982. 99 p.

Hall, Richard, ed. *South West Africa (Namibia): Proposals for Action.* London: Africa Bureau, 1970. 45 p.

Hellberg, Carl-J. *Namibia.* Stockholm: Verbum, 1975. 46 p.

Horrell, Muriel. *South-West Africa.* Johannesburg, S.A.: Institute of Race Relations, 1967. (viii), 94 p.

Hovey, Gail. *Namibia's Stolen Wealth: North American Investment and South African Occupation.* New York, N.Y.: Africa Fund, 1982. iv, 52 p.

Ilanga-Nyonschi, Medard. *Le Capital international et ses effets en Namibie.* Sherbrooke, Quebec: Editions Naaman, 1978. 244 p.

Indian Society of International Law. *The Question of South-West Africa: Documents and Comments.* New Delhi, 1966. vii, 186 p.

International Conference in Support of the Struggle of the Namibian People for Independence, 1983, Paris, France. *Report of the International Conference in Support of the Struggle of the Namibian People for Independence, Paris, 25–29 April 1983.* New York: United Nations, 1983. ix, 171 p.

International Conference on Sanctions Against South Africa, 1981, Paris, France. *International Conference on Sanctions Against South Africa, UNESCO House, Paris, 20–27 May 1981.* New York United Nations Centre Against Apartheid, 1982. 2 v.

———. *Paris Declaration on Sanctions Against South Africa.* New York: United Nations, 1982. 13 p.

———. *Report of the International Conference on Sanctions Against South Africa: Paris, 20–27 May 1981.* New York: United Nations, 1981. vi, 143 p.

International Court of Justice. *Legal Consequences for States of the Continued Presence of South Africa in Namibia (South West Africa), Notwithstanding Security Council Resolution 276 (1970) (Conséquences juridiques pour les Etats de la présence continue de l'Afrique du Sud en Namibie (Sud-Ouest africain) nonobstant la résolution 276 (1970) du Conseil de sécurité).* The Hague, 1971. 2 v.

International Labour Office. *Labour and Discrimination in Namibia.* Geneva: International Labour Office, 1977. viii, 126 p.

International Seminar on the Role of Transnational Corporations in Namibia, 1982, Washington, D.C. *Document(s): no. NS–1–44/International Seminar on the Role of Transnational Corporations in Namibia, Washington, D.C., November 29–December 2, 1982.* Organized by the American Committee on Africa with the support of the United Nations Council for Namibia. New York: The Committee, 1982.

Investment in SWA/Namibia. Windhoek, SWA/Namibia: First National Development Corp. of SWA, 1981. 24 p.

Iordanov, Emil. *Namibiia—trudniiat put kum svobodata.* Sofia: Partizdat, 1982. 100 p.

Jacobs, Walter Darnell. *A Special Study of South West Africa in Law and Politics.* New York: American-African Affairs Association, 1966. 20 p.

Jaster, Robert S. *Southern Africa in Conflict: Implications for U.S. Policies in the 1980s.* Washington: American Enterprise Institute for Public Policy Research, 1982. 48 p.

Kane-Berman, John Stuart. *Contract Labour in South West Africa.* Johannesburg: South African Institute of Race Relations, 1972. (2), 37, xxxii p.

Karina, Mburumba. *The Democratic Option in Namibia.* Washington: Institute on Religion and Democracy, 1984. 11 p.

———. *Namibia, the Making of a Nation.* New York: Books in Focus, 1982. 314 p.

Kesselly, Edward B. *South-West Africa and New Guinea: A Systems Approach.* Geneva, 1967. 115 leaves.

Konrat, Georg vvon. *Passport to Truth: Inside South West Africa: An Astounding Story of Oppression.* London, New York: W. H. Allen, 1972. xii, 241 p.

Kramer, Reed. *Tsumeb: A Profile of United States Contribution to Underdevelopment in Namibia: A Report.* New York: Corporate Information Center, National Council of Churches, 1973. 35 p.

Kuntze, Lisa. *Die Macht der Diamanten: sechsundsechzig, ernste, heitere und tragische Diamantengeschichten aus Sudwestafrika.* Windhoek: Verlag der SWA Wissenschaftlichen Gesellschaft, 1983. 164 p.

———. *Was halt Euch denn hier fest?: 55 Lebensgeschichten aus Sudwestafrika/Namibia.* Windhoek: Verlag der SWA Wissenschaftlichen Gesellschaft, 1982. 228 p.

Labour Party (Great Britain). Executive Committee. *Namibia: A Statement.* London: Labour Party, 1976. 16 p.

Landis, Elizabeth. *Namibia: The Beginning of Disengagement.* Denver: University of Denver, 1970. 47 p.

———. *Namibian Liberation: Self-Determination, Law, and Politics.* New York: Episcopal Churchmen for South Africa, c1982. 15 p.

Leistner, Erich, et. al. *Namibia/SWA Prospectus.* Pretoria: African Institute of South Africa, 1980. vi, 66 p.

Lejeune, Anthony. *The Case for South West Africa.* London: Tom Stacey Ltd., 1971. 245 (4) p.

Liberia. *South West Africa Case (Liberia versus the Union of South Africa).* Memorial submitted by the Government of Liberia. The Hague, 1961. vi, 3–180 p.

Louw, W. *Owambo.* Sandton, South Africa: Southern African Freedom Foundation, (1971–). 91 p.

Lund, Wenda. *Rosing und das üllegale Geschaft mit dem Namibia-Uran: eine Untersuchung zur grossten Uranmine der Welt und ihrer strategischen Bedeutung.* Cologne: Pahl-Rugenstein, 1984. iv, 208 p.

Mader, Julius. *Neo-colonialist Practices of the Federal Republic of Germany in Relation to Namibia.* Berlin: Solidaritatskomitee der DDR, 1978. 27 p.

Malan, J. S. *Peoples of South West Africa/Namibia.* Pretoria: HAUM, 1980. 113 p.

Manchester Nonviolent Action Group. *Namibia, a Call to Be Answered: The Facts About South Africa's Illegal Occupation of South West Africa.* London: Housmans for Manchester Nonviolent Action Group, 1972. (3), 26 p.

Massacre at Kassinga: Climax of Pretoria's All-Out Campaign Against the Namibian Resistance. Luanda: South West Africa People's Organization, 1978. 26 p.

May, Edward C. *Report of the Wingspread Conference on Namibia, Convened by the Lutheran Council in the U.S.A. and the Johnson Foundation.* Racine, Wis.: The Foundation, 1976. 25 p.

Megevand, Beatrice. *La questione della Namibia (Africa di Sud Ovvest.* Milan: A. Giuffre, 1982. viii, 268 p.

Mines and Independence. London: Catholic Institute for International Relations; New York: Copies available from Africa Fund, 1983. 155 p.

Mokobane, Simon Rapule. *A Select Bibliography on South West Africa/Namibia.* Johannesburg: South African Institute of Race Relations, 1980. 25 p.

Molnar, Thomas Steven. *Spotlight on South West Africa.* New York: American-African Affairs Association, 1966. 18 p.

Murray, Roger, et al. *The Role of Foreign Firms in Namibia: Studies on External Investment and Black Workers Conditions in Namibia.* London: Africa Publications Trust. Distributed by Study Project on External Investment in South Africa and Namibia, 1974. 220 p.

Namibia. K } benhavn: Namibia–75, 1978. 16 p.

Namibia and the Nordic countries. Uppsala: Scandinavian Institute of African Studies, 1981. 44 p.

Namibia in the 1980's. London: Catholic Institute for International Relations. British Council of Churches, 1981. 84 p.

Namibia Revolution. Cairo: Permanent Secretariat of the Afro-Asian Peoples' Solidarity Organization, 1971. 62 p.

Namibia: SWAPO Fights for Freedom. Edited by Liberation Support Movement. Oakland, Cal.: LSM Information Center, 1978. 124 p.

Namibia: The Crisis in United States Policy Toward Southern Africa. Africa Committee, National Council of Churches of Christ in the U.S.A. Washington, D.C.: TransAfrica, 1983. vi, 49 p.

Namibia: The Facts. London: International Defence and Aid Fund, 1980. 100 p.

The Namibian Documentation. 1971.

Ndadi, Vinnia. *Breaking Contract: The Story of Vinnia Ndadi.* Edited by Dennis Mercer. Richmond, B.C.: LSM Information Center, 1974. 116 p.

Newman, Anne, and Bowers, Cathy. *Foreign Investment in South Africa and Namibia: A Directory of U.S., Canadian and British Corporations Operating in South Africa and Namibia With a Survey of the 100 Largest Bank Holding Companies and Their Practices and Policies on Lending to South Africa.* Washington: Investor Responsibility Research Center, 1984. 279 p.

Obozuwa, A. Ukiomogbe. *The Namibian Question: Legal and Political As-*

pects. Benin City, Nigeria: Ethiope Publishing Corp., 1973. xviii, 256 p.

O'Callaghan, Marion. *Namibia: The Effects of Apartheid on Culture and Education.* Paris: Unesco, 1977. 169 p.

O'Linn, Bryan. *Die Toekoms van Suidwes-Afrika gebou op die werklikheid.* Windhoek: Federale Publikasies, 1974. iv, 128 p.

———. *Die Zukunft Sudwestafrikas in realistischer Sicht.* Windhoek: Federale Publikasies, 1976. 200 p.

Parker, Frank J. *South Africa: Lost Opportunities.* Lexington, Mass.: Lexington Books, 1983. xii, 290 p.

Plunder of Namibian Uranium: Major Findings of the Hearings on Namibian Uranium Held by the United Nations Council for Namibia in July 1980. New York: United Nations, 1982. 35 p.

Poewe, Karla O. *The Namibian Herero: A History of the Psychosocial Disintegration and Survival.* New York: E. Mellen Press, 1985.

Policies and Practices of Transnational Corporations Regarding Their Activities in South Africa and Namibia. United Nations Centre on Transnational Corporations. New York: United Nations, 1984. iv, 55 p.

The Population Groups of South West Africa: Facts and Figures. Windhoek, South West Africa: Afrikaans-Deutsche Kulturgemeinschaft, 1978-1980. 2 v.

Prinsloo, D.S. *SWA/Namibia: Towards a Negotiated Settlement.* Pretoria: Foreign Affairs Association, 1977. 38 p.

Remember Kassinga, and Other Papers on Political Prisoners and Detainees in Namibia. London: International Defence and Aid Fund, 1981. 52 p.

Report on Namibia, Pretoria, South Africa. Southern African Catholic Bishop's Conference, 1982. 40 p.

Rittershaus, Wilhelm. *Sudafrika geht uns alle an.* Reifnitz: Eigenver, 1976. 154 p.

Rocha, Gejsa Maria. *In Search of Namibian Independence: The Limitations of the United Nations.* Boulder, Colo.: Westview Press, 1984. xi, 192 p.

Rotberg, Robert I., ed. *Namibia: Political and Economic Prospects.* Lexington, Mass.: Lexington Books, 1983. viii, 133 p.

———. *Namibia: Politics, Ecology, and Society. Final Report.* Washington: African-American Scholars Council, 1977. 62 leaves.

Rubin, Neville N. *Labour and Discrimination in Namibia.* Geneva: International Labour Office, 1977. 126 p.

———. *Proposals for Effective International Action Concerning Namibia.* Geneva: International University Exchange Fund, 1971. 11 p.

Sagay, Itsejuwa Esanjumi. *The Legal Aspects of the Namibian Dispute.* Ile Ife, Nigeria: University of Ife Press, 1975. xxxii, 402 p.

Saunders, Christopher, ed. *Perspectives on Namibia, Past and Present.* Rondebosch, South Africa: Centre for African Studies, University of Capetown, 1983. 162 p.

Saxena, Suresh Chandra. *Namibia, Challenge to the United Nations*. Delhi: Sundeep Prakashan, 1978. vii, 316 p.

Schneider-Barthold, Wolfgang. *Namibia's Economic Potential and Existing Economic Ties with the Republic of South Africa*. Berlin: German Development Institute, 1977. ii, 93 p.

Schoeman, Elna. *The Namibian Issue, 1920–1980: A Select and Annotated Bibliography*. Boston, Mass.: G.K. Hall, 1982. xxix, 247 p.

———. *South West Africa/Namibia: An International Issue 1920–1977: A Select Bibliography*. Johannesburg: South African Institute of International Affairs, 1978. xviii, 161 p.

Serfontein, J. H. P. *Namibia*. Randburg, South Africa: Fokus Suid Publishers, 1976. xv, 433 p.

Shack, William A. *The Multi-Ethnic Factor in Namibia: Final Report*. Washington: African-American Scholars Council, 1977. ir, 65 leaves.

Shipanga, Andreas. *Interview With Andreas Shipanga*. Interviewed by Dennis Mercer. Richmond, B.C.: LSM Information Center, 1973. 27 p.

Short, Joseph N. *Politics in Namibia: Final Report*. Washington: African-American Scholars Council, 1977. 35 leaves.

Silagi, Michael. *Von Deutsch-Sudwest zu Namibia: Wesen und Wandlungen des volkerrechtlichen Mandats*. Ebelsbach: R. Gremer, 1977. ix, 165 p.

Simon, David. *Contemporary Namibia, the Political Geography of Decolonization*. Oxford: School of Geography, University of Oxford, 1983. 37 p.

Sjoquist, Eric. *En minut i tolv: Sydafrika och Namibia i narbild*. Stockholm: Atlantis, 1979. (5) p., p. 13–187.

Slonim, Solomon. *South West Africa and the United Nations: An International Mandate in Dispute*. Baltimore: John Hopkins University Press, 1973. xix, 409 p.

South Africa. Dept. of Foreign Affairs. *South West Africa: Measures Taken to Combat Terrorism. Text of Letter Dated 15th February, 1968, and Annexures, Addressed to the Secretary-General of the United Nations by the South African Minister of Foreign Affairs*. Cape Town, 1968. 28 p.

South Africa. Dept. of Information. *Ethiopia and Liberia Versus South Africa: An Official Account of the Contentious Proceedings on South West Africa before the International Court of Justice at the Hague, 1960–1966*. Pretoria: Department of Information, 1966. ix, 303 p.

South West Africa Advisory Opinion 1971: A Study in International Adjudication. Pretoria: Dept. of Foreign Affairs of the Republic of South Africa, 1972. 136 p.

South West Africa: Basic Documents, 30 January 1976 to May 1979. Compiled and issued by the Department of Foreign Affairs of the Republic of South Africa. Pretoria: The Department, 1979. viii, 281 p.

South West Africa Cases: Ethiopia and Liberia Versus the Republic of South Africa. Reply of the Governments Ethhiopia and Liberia. Hague: International Court of Justice, 1964. xii, 396 p.

South West Africa Peoples Organisation. *The Political Programme of the South West Africa People's Organization (SWAPO) of Namibia.* Dar es Salaam: SWAPO, 197–). 10 leaves.

————. Central Committee. *The Declaration of the Central Committee of the South West Africa People's Organization (SWAPO) of Namibia, Adopted by Its Second Annual Meeting Held at Gabela, P. R. of Angola, 4-7 January 1979.* Lusaka: SWAPO, Dept. of Information and Publicity, 1979. 4 leaves.

————. Dept. of Information and Publicity. *To Be Born a Nation: The Liberation Struggle of Namibia.* Department of Information and Publicity, SWAPO of Namibia. London: Zed Press, 1981. v, 357 p.

South West Africa: Problems and Alternatives. Cape Town: Centre for Extra-Mural Studies, University of Cape Town, 1977. 1 v.

Steenkamp, Willem. *Borderstrike!: South Africa into Angola.* Durban, Pretoria: Woburn, Mass.: Butterworths, 1983. 266 p.

Strauss, F.J. *S.W.A. vir dir wolwe?* Windhoek: Eros, 1981. 150 p.

SWAPO Students' Seminar, Moscow, 1975. *The Role of the Youth and Students in the National Liberation Struggle: SWAPO Students' Seminar, Moscow, January 26–29, 1975.* Dar es Salaam: South West Africa People's Organisation, 1975–1978. 49 p.

Symposium on the Exploitation of Blacks in South Africa and Namibia and on Prison Conditions in South African Jails, Maseru, Lesotho, 17–22 July 1978. Organized by the United Nations Division of Human Rights in co-operation with the Government of Lesotho. Geneva: United Nations, 1978. ii, 34 p.

Thomas, Wolfgang H. *Economic Development in Namibia: Toward Acceptable Development Strategies for Independent Namibia.* New Brunswick, N.J.: Transaction Books, 1985.

Tøj til Afrika (Society). *Befrielseskampen i Namibia.* København, Vibevej 7, 2400 NV: Tøj Til Afrika, 1980. 60 p.

To Honour Women's Day: Profiles of Leading Women in the South African and Namibian Liberation Struggles. London: International Defence and Aid Fund for Southern Africa, 1981. 56 p.

Totemeyer, Gerhard. *Namibia Old and New: Traditional and Modern Leaders in Ovamboland.* London: C. Hurst, 1978. x, 257 p.

————. *South West Africa, Namibia: Facts, Attitudes, Assessment, and Prospects.* Randburg, South Africa: Fokus Suid Publishers; London: Distributed by R. Collings, 1977. x, 321 p.

Ulanovskaia, Irina Arkad evna. *Namibiia—bor ba prodolzhaetsia*. Moscow: Znanie, 1980. 64 p.

United Nations. *United Nations Resolutions on Namibia, 1946–1978*. Compiled by A.D. Evborokhai. Lusaka, Zambia: United Nations Institute for Namibia, 1980. 2 v.

United Nations. Commission on Human Rights. *The Adverse Consequences for the Enjoyment of Human Rights of Political, Military, Economic and Other Forms of Assistance Given to the Colonial and Racist Regimes in Southern Africa* (E/CN.4/Sub.2/371), 1976. 54 p.

United Nations. Commission on Human Rights. *Report of the ad hoc Working Group of Experts Prepared in Accordance with Resolution 7 (XXVII) of the Commission on Human Rights* (E/CN.4/1076), 1972. 28 p.

United Nations. Council for Namibia. *Addendum to the Report*. General Assembly, Official Records, 29th sess., Suppl. no. 24A. 29 p.

United Nations. Council for Namibia. *Political Developments Related to Namibia* (A/AC.131/90), 1982. 24 p.

United Nations. Council for Namibia. *Report*. General Assembly, Official Records, 25th sess., Suppl. no. 24., 1970, 51 p.

United Nations. Council for Namibia. *Report*. General Assembly, Official Records, 26th sess., Suppl. no. 24., 1971. 87 p.

United Nations. Council for Namibia. *Report*. General Assembly, Official Records, 28th sess., Suppl. no. 24., 1974, 117 p.

United Nations. Council for Namibia. *Report*. General Assembly, Official Records, 31st sess., Suppl. no. 24., 1976. 2 v.

United Nations. Council for Namibia. *Report of the Council's Mission to Africa, 1970* (A/AC.131/20), 1970. 37 p.

United Nations. Council for Namibia. *Report of the Mission of Consultation of the United Nations Council for Namibia to Cuba, Panama, Jamaica, Barbados and Trinidad and Tobago* (A/35/338), 1980. 44 p.

United Nations. Council for Namibia. *Report of the Mission of Consultation of the United Nations Council for Namibia to the Libyan Arab Jamahiriya, Kuwait and Iraq* (A/35/364), 1980. 1, 31, 6 p.

United Nations. Council for Namibia. *Report on the Activities of Foreign Economic Interests Operating in Namibia* (A/AC.131/115), 1984. 34 p.

United Nations. Council for Namibia. *Report*. General Assembly, Official Records, 27th sess., Suppl. no. 24, 1972. 52 p.

United Nations. Council for Namibia. *Report*. General Assembly, Official Records, 29th sess., Suppl. no. 24, 1974. 60 p.

United Nations. Council for Namibia. *Report*. General Assembly, Official Records, 27th sess., Suppl. no. 24l, 1972. 61 p.

United Nations. Council for Namibia. *Report*. General Assembly, Official Records, 29th sess., Suppl. no. 24, 1975. 75 p.

United Nations. General Assembly. *Letter Dated 22 January 1976 from the Permanent Representative of the Libyan Arab Republic to the United Nations Addressed to the Secretary-General* (A/31/45), 1976. 12 p.

United Nations. General Assembly. *Letter Dated 6 June 1977 from the Chairman of the Special Committee on the Situation with Regard to the Implementation of the Declaration on the Granting of Independence to Colonial Countries and Peoples and the Acting President of the United Nations Council for Namibia* (A/32/109/Rev. 1), 1977. 1 v.

United Nations. General Assembly. Special Committee on the Situation with Regard to the Implementation of the Declaration on the Granting of Independence to Colonial Countries and Peoples. *Activities of Foreign Economic and Other Interests Which Are Impeding the Implementation of the Declaration on the Granting of Independence to Colonial Countries and Peoples in Southern Rhodesia, Namibia and Territories Under Portuguese Domination and in All Other Territories Under Colonial Domination and Efforts to Eliminate Colonialism, Apartheid and Racial Discrimination in Southern Africa: Report* (A/8148/Add. 1), 1970. 85 p.

United Nations. General Assembly. Special Committee on the Situation with Regard to the Implementation of the Declaration on Granting of Independence to Colonial Countries and Peoples. *Report . . . [covering its work during 1972]* (A/8723 (Part II), (Add. 2), (Part III), 1972. 45, 50, 169 p.

United Nations. General Assembly. Special Committee on the Situation with Regard to the Implementation of the Declaration on the Granting of Independence to Colonial Countries and Peoples. *Report . . . [covering its work during 1975]* (A/10023 (Part III)), 1975. 61 p.

United Nations. General Assembly. Special Committee on the Situation with Regard to the Implementation of the Declaration on the Granting of Independence to Colonial Countries and Peoples. *Report . . . [covering its work during 1976]* (A/31/23 (Part III), (Part IV), (Add. 3)), 1976. 22, 6, 18, 15, 9, 3, 3, 43 p.

United Nations. General Assembly. Special Committee on the Situation with Regard to the Implementation of the Declaration on the Granting of Independence to Colonial Countries and Peoples. *Report* (A/10023/Add.3), 1975. 42 p.

United Nations. General Assembly. Special Committee on the Situation with Regard to the Implementation of the Declaration on the Granting of Independence to Colonial Countries and Peoples. *Report* (A/9623/Add.3), 1974. 25 p.

United Nations. General Assembly. Special Committee on the Situation with Regard to the Implementation of the Declaration on the Granting of Independence to Colonial Countries and Peoples. *Report* (A/8023/Add.2), 1970. 39 p.

United Nations. Office of Public Information. *A Principle in Torment: III, the United Nations and Namibia.* (E.71.I.4), 1971. 44 p.

United Nations. Office of Public Information. *A Trust Betrayed, Namibia* (OPI/528), 1974. 43 p.

United Nations. Secretariat. *Activities of Transnational Corporations in Southern Africa and the Extent of Their Collaboration with the Illegal Regimes in the Area: Report* (E/C.10/26), 1977. 53 p.

United Nations. Secretariat. *Namibia: Working Paper* (A/AC.109/L.686), 1971. 37 p.

United Nations. Secretariat. *Namibia: Working Paper* (A/AC.109/L.761), 1972. 31 p.

United Nations. Secretariat. *Namibia: Working Paper Prepared by the Secretariat* (A/AC.109/653), 1981. 29 p.

United Nations. Secretariat. *Organization of Work: Relevant Resolutions and Decisions of the General Assembly and the United Nations Council for Namibia* (A/AC.131/L.5), 1973, 17 p.

United Nations. Secretary-General, 1961–1971 (Thant). *Question of Namibia and United Nations Fund for Namibia: Report* (A/8473), 1971. 30 p.

United Nations. Secretary-General, 1961–1971 (Thant). *Report . . . in Pursuance of Resolution 269 (1969) Adopted by the Security Council at its 149th Meeting on 12 August 1969 Concerning the Situation in Namibia.* Security Council, Official Records, 24th year, Social Suppl. no. 2, 19770. 142 p.

United Nations. Secretary-General, 1961–1971 (Thant). *Review of Multilateral Treaties to Which South Africa Became A Party, and Which Either By Direct Reference or on the Basis of Relevant Provisions of International Law Might be Considered to Apply to Namibia* (S/10288), 1971. 23 p.

United Nations. Secretary-General, 1972–1981 (Waldheim). *Compliance of Member States with the United Nations Resolutions and Decisions Relating to Namibia, Taking into Account the Advisory Opinion of the International Court of Justice of 21 June 1971: Report* (A/AC.131/370), 1975. 54 p.

United Nations. Secretary-General, 1972–1981 (Waldheim). *The Effects of Apartheid on the Status of Women in South Africa, Namibia and Southern Rhodesia: Report* (E/CN.6/619), 1978. 28 p.

United Nations. Secretary-General, 1972–1981 (Waldheim). *Elimination of All Forms of Racial Discrimination: Decade for Action to Combat Racism and Racial Discrimination: Report* (A/31/236), 1976. 12 p.

United Nations. Secretary-General, 1972–1981 (Waldheim). *Question of Namibia* (A/10229), 1975. 8, 2 p.

United Nations. Secretary-General, 1972–1981 (Waldheim). *Question of Namibia: Report* (A/9225), 1973. 7 p.

United Nations. Secretary-General, 1972–1981 (Waldheim). *Question of Namibia: United Nations Fund for Namibia* (A/8841), 1972. 6 p.

United Nations. Secretary-General, 1972–1981 (Waldheim). *Question of Namibia: United Nations Fund for Namibia* (A/9725), 1974. 9 p.

United Nations. Secretary-General, 1972–1981 (Waldheim). *Report by the Secretary-General on the Implementation of Security Council Resolution 301 (1971)* (S/10708), 1972. 8 p.

United Nations. Secretary-General, 1971–1981 (Waldheim). *Report by the Secretary-General on the Implementation of Security Council Resolution 309 (1972) Concerning the Question of Namibia* (S/10738), 1972. 15 p.

United Nations. Secretary-General, 1972–1981 (Waldheim). *Report... on the Implementation of Security Council Resolution 323 (1972) Concerning the Question of Namibia* (S/10921), 1973. 7 p.

United Nations. Secretary-General, 1972–1981 (Waldheim). *Report... on the Implementation of Security Resolution 319 (1972) Concerning the Question of Namibia* (S/10832), 1972. 23 p.

United Nations. Security Council. *Letter Dated 27 January 1976 from the Permanent Representative of South Africa to the United Nations Addressed to the Secretary-General* (A/11948/Add. 1), 1976. 70 p.

United Nations. Security Council. Ad Hoc Sub-Committee on Namibia. *Report* (S/10330), 1971. 26 p.

United States. Congress. House. Committee on Foreign Affairs. *Africa: Observations on the Impact of American Foreign Policy and Development Programs in Six African Countries. Report of a Congressional Study Mission to Zimbabwe, South Africa, Kenya, Somalia, Angola and Nigeria, August 4-22, 1981, Submitted to the Committee on Foreign Affairs,* 97th Cong., 2d sess., 1982. 82 p.

United States. Congress. House. Committee on Foreign Affairs. Subcommittee on Africa. *Critical Developments in Namibia. Hearings before the subcommittee on Africa of the Committee on Foreign Affairs,* 93d Cong., 2d sess., February 21 and April 4, 1974. iv, 305 p.

United States. Congress. House. Committee on Foreign Affairs. Subcommittee on Africa. *The Current Situation in Namibia. Hearing before the Subcommittee on Africa of the Committee on Foreign Affairs,* 96th Cong., 1st sess., May 7, 1979. iii, 36 p.

United States. Congress. House. Committee on Foreign Affairs. Subcommittee on Africa. *Namibia and Regional Destabilization in Southern Africa. Hearing before the Subcommittee on Africa of the Committee on Foreign Affairs,* 98th Cong., 1st sess., February 15, 1983. iv, 35 p.

United States. Congress. House. Committee on Foreign Affairs. Subcommittee on Africa. *Namibia Update. Hearing before the Subcommittee on Africa of the Committee on Foreign Affairs*, 96th Cong., 2d sess., September 9, 1980. iv, 35 p.

United States. Congress. House. Committee on Foreign Affairs. Subcommittee on Africa. *Regional Destabilization in Southern Africa. Hearing*, 97th Cong., 2nd sess., December 8, 1982. 175 p.

United States. Congress. House. Committee on Foreign Affairs. Subcommittee on Africa. *U.S. Policy Toward Namibia, Spring 1981. Hearing before the Subcommittee on Africa of the Committee on Foreign Affairs*, 97th Cong., 1st sess., June 17, 1981. iii, 41 p.

United States. Congress. House. Committee on Foreign Affairs. Subcommittee on Africa. *United States Policy Toward Southern Africa: Focus on Namibia, Angola, and South Africa.Hearing and markup*, 97th Cong., 1st sess., September 16, 1981. 61 p.

United States. Congress. House. Committee on International Relations. Subcommittee on International Organizations. *Namibia, the United Nations and U.S. Policy. Hearings before the Subcommittee on International Organizations of the Committee on International Relations*, 94th Cong., 2d sess., August 24 and 27, 1976. iii, 258 p.

United States. Congress. House. Committee on International Relations. Subcommittee on International Resources, Food, and Energy. *Resources in Namibia: Implications for U.S. Policy. Hearings before the Subcommittee on International Resources, Food and Energy of the Committee on International Relations*, 94th Cong., June 10, 1975 and May 13, 1976. iv, 165 p.

United States. Congress. House. Committee on the District of Columbia. Subcommittee on Fiscal Affairs and Health. *South Africa Divestment. Hearing and Markups before the Subcommittee on Fiscal Affairs and Health of the Committee on the District of Columbia*, 98th Cong., 2d sess., January 31 and February 7, 1984. iv, 520 p.

United States. Congress. Senate. Committee on Foreign Relations. Subcommittee on African Affairs. *Namibia. Hearing before the Subcommittee on African Affairs of the Committee on Foreign Relations*, 96th Cong., 1st sess., June 25, 1979. iii, 50 p.

United States. Congress. Senate. Committee on the Judiciary. Subcommittee on Security and Terrorism. *The Role of the Soviet Union, Cuba and East Germany in Fomenting Terrorism in Southern Africa—Addendum. Hearings*, 97th Cong., 2d sess., 1982. 967 p.

Van der Vyver, J. D. *South West Africa/Namibia: A Symposium*. Held by the Institute at Jan Smuts House on 28 January, 1976. Braamfontein: South African Institute of International Affairs, 1976. 23 p.

Van Rooyen, Ina, ed. *SWA/Namibia Today*. Windhoek: SWA/Namibia Information Service, 1980. 120 p.

Van Wyk, Jacques Theodore. *The United Nations, South West Africa, and the Law.* Cape Town: University of Cape Town, 1968. 30 p.

Venter, Thomas Denis. *SWA/Namibia, Prospects for Coalition-Formation.* Pretoria: Africa Institute of South Africa, 1978. 29 p.

Wagner-Robertz, Dagmar Johanna. *Namibia, a Unique UN Responsibility: Highlights of United Nations Action in Support of Freedom and Independence for Namibia.* New York: United Nations Dept. of Public Information, 1980. 30 p.

What One Should Know About South West Africa: Facts and Figures. Windhoek, South West Africa: Afrikaans-Deutsche Kulturgemeinschaft, 1978. 24 p.

Winter, Colin O'Brien. *Namibia.* Grand Rapids, Mich.: Eerdmans, 1977. v, 234 p.

Ya-Otto, John. *Battlefront Namibia: An Autobiography.* Westport, Conn.: L. Hill & Co., 1981. 151 p.

Articles

Adelman, Kenneth. "Western Policy in Southern Africa," *Current History* 78 (March 1980): 124–26.

Alexandrowicz, Charles H. "The Juridical Expression of the Sacred Trust of Civilization." *American Journal of International Law* 65 (January 1971): 149–59.

Amery, Julian. "The Crisis in Southern Africa: Policy Options for London and Washington." *Policy Review* 2 (Fall 1977): 89–111.

Anderson, David. "America in Africa, 1981." *Foreign Affairs, America and the World* 60 (1982): 658–85.

Austin, George. "World Council of Churches' Program to Combat Racism." *Conflict Studies* 105 (1979): 20 p.

Barrat, John. "Southern Africa: A South African View." *Foreign Affairs* 55 (October 1976): 147–68.

Best, Alan C. B. and Deblij, Harm J. "Namibia: Political Geography of a Coveted Prize." *Focus* 26 (January-February 1976): 1–17.

Bissell, Richard E. "Stability and Security in Southern Africa." *International Security Review* 6 (Summer 1981): 173–88.

Botha, R.F. "Let Nobody Doubt Our Will to Resist." *Worldview* 20 (September 1977): 10–16.

Buehrig, Edward H. "The Resolution-Based International Agency." *Political Studies* 29 (June 1981): 217–31.

Butcher, Goler Teal. "Reflections on U.S. Policy Towards Namibia." *Issue* 4 (Fall 1974): 59–62.

Butterfield, Ian. "Toward a Namibian Settlement." *Backgrounder* 167 (1982): 10 p.

Caminada, Jerome. "Change in Southern Africa." *Ditchley Journal* 7 (Spring 1980): 5–13.

Chimutengwende, Chenhamo C. "The Media and the State in South African Politics." *Black Scholar* 10 (September 1978): 44–57.

Claude, Patrice. "Namibia and Independence: History Is With Us." *Manchester Guardian Weekly* 125 (August 23, 1981): 12.

Clough, Michael. "United States Policy in Southern Africa."*Current History* 83 (March 1984): 97.

Coker, Christopher. "South Africa: A New Military Role in Southern Africa 1969–82." *Survival* 25 (March-April 1983): 59–67.

―――. "The United States and National Liberation in Southern Africa." *African Affairs* 78 (July 1979): 319–30.

Collet, Sue. "The Human Factor in the Economic Development of Namibia." *Optima* 28 (January 1980): 191.

Copley, Gregory. "Where Lion Roam No More." *Defense and Foreign Affairs* 12 (September 1984): 8.

Crocker, Chester A.; Greszes, Mario; and Henderson, Robert. "Southern Africa: A U.S. Policy for the '80s." *Freedom At Issue* 58 (November-December 1980): 11–18.

―――. "A U.S. Policy for the '80s." *Africa Report* 26 (January-February 1981): 7–14.

Dale, Richard. "The Armed Forces as an Instrument of South African Policy in Namibia." *Journal of Modern African Studies* 18 (March 1980): 57–71.

―――. "Political, Economic, and Security Changes in Botswana, Namibia, and South Africa, 1966–79." *Parameters* 9 (September 1979): 56–69.

―――. "The Political Futures of South West Africa and Namibia." *World Affairs* 134 (Spring 1972): 325–43.

―――. "South Africa and Namibia: Changing the Guard and Guarded Change." *Current History* 76 (March 1979): 101.

Dedial, Jurg. "Drought and Doubt in Namibia." *Swiss Review of World Affairs* 32 (June 1982): 23.

DeSt. Jorre, John. "South Africa: Is Change Coming?" *Foreign Affairs* 60 (Fall 1981): 106–22.

DeVilliers, W. Brucker. "The Namibian Drama." *Africa Institute Bulletin* 16 (1978): 136–55.

Dodd, Norman L. "African Navies South of the Sahara." *United States Naval Institute Proceedings* 110 (March 1984): 55–59.

Dugard, John. "The Nuclear Test Cases and the South West Africa Cases: Some Realism About the International Judicial Decision." *Virginia Journal of International Law* 16 (Spring 1976): 463–504.

———. "South West Africa and the 'Terrorist Trial.' *American Journal of International Law* 64 (January 1970): 19–41.

Du Pisani, Andre. "Namibia: The Quest for Legitimacy." *Politeia* 2 (1983): 43–51.

"Facts and Figures on SWA." *Africa Institute Bulletin* 16 (1978): 165–75.

Finger, Seymour Maxwell. "Andrew Young at the UN." *Foreign Service Journal* 57 (July-August 1980): 17.

Geyser, O. "Detente in Southern Africa." *African Affairs* 75 (April 1976): 182–207.

Gordon, David F. "Conflict Resolution in Southern Africa: Why Namibia Is Not Another Zimbabwe." *Issue: A Journal of Africanist Opinion* 12 (Fall-Winter 1982): 37–45.

Gordon, Edward. "Old Orthodoxies Amid New Experiences: The South West Africa (Namibia) Litigation and the Uncertain Jurisprudence of the International Court of Justice."*Denver Journal of International Law and Policy* 1 (Fall 1971): 65–92.

Gross, Steven R. "The United Nations, Self-Determination and the Namibia Opinions." *Yale Law Journal* 82 (January 1973): 533–58.

Grotpeter, John. "Changing South Africa." *Current History* 78 (March 1980): 119.

Grundy, Kenneth. "Namibia in International Politics."*Current History* 81 (March 1982): 101.

Gupta, Anirudha. "Issues in Southern Africa."*International Studies* 17 (January-March 1978): 1–25.

Gutteridge, William. "South Africa: Strategy for Survival?" *Conflict Studies* 131 (1981): 32 p.

Hallett, Robin. "The South African Intervention in Angola, 1975–76." *African Affairs* 77 (July 1978): 347–86.

Henriksen, Thomas H. "Namibia: A Comparison With Anti-Portuguese Insurgency." *Round Table* 278 (April 1980): 184–94.

Hevener, Natalie K. "The 1971 South-West Africa Opinion: A New International Juridical Philosophy." *International and Comparative Law Quarterly* 24 (October 1975): 791–810.

Higgins, Rosalyn. "The Advisory Opinion on Namibia: Which UN Resolutions Are Binding Under Article 25 of the Charter?" *International and Comparative Law Quarterly* 21 (April 1972): 270–86.

Hitchens, Christopher. "Namibia—The Birth of a Nation."*New Statesman* 96 (November 1978): 572.

Husain, Azim. "The Diversion of U.S. Ocean Cargo Through Canadian Ports: An Evaluation of the Need For Regulations." *George Washington Journal of International Law and Economics* 17 (1982): 167–204.

Hynning, Clifford J. "The Future of South West Africa: A Plebiscite?" *American Journal of International Law* 65 (September 1971): 144–67.

"Interviews With Sam Nujoma and Thabo Nbeki." *Africa News* 23 (July 1984): 5–9.

James, H. E.; Boydell, D. W.; and Simonsen, H. A. "South African Uranium Industry Plans For Expansion." *Nuclear Engineering International* 23 (November 1978): 42–45.

Janke, Peter. "Southern Africa: New Horizons." *Conflict Studies* 73 (1976): 20 p.

Jaster, Robert S. "A Regional Security Role for Africa's Front-Line States: Experience and Prospects." *Adelphi Prospects* 180 (1983): 45 p.

Jenkins, Simon. "Destabilisation in Southern Africa." *Economist* 288 (July 1983): 19–28.

Jinadu, L. Adele. "South West Africa: A Study in the 'Sacred Trust' Thesis." *African Studies Review* 14 (December 1971): 369–88.

Jones, Emma Coleman. "Limitations of the International Legal Mechanism: Namibia (South West Africa), a Case Study." *Howard Law Journal* 17 (1972): 637–60.

Jordan-Walker, Deneice C. "Settlement of the Namibian Dispute: The United States Role in Lieu of U.N. Sanctions."*Case Western Reserve Journal of International Law* 14 (Summer 1982): 543–71.

Kahn, E. J., Jr. "Who Cares?...We Do!" *New Yorker* 55 (June 25, 1979): 60–88.

Kane-Berman, John; Walker, Steve; and Foy, Colm. "The Spectre of a Free Namibia." *New Statesman* 102 (September 1981): 6–8.

Kaunda, Kenneth. "Kenneth Kaunda, President of Zambia." *Africa Report* 28 (May-June 1983): 4–7.

Kennan, George F. "Hazardous Courses in Southern Africa." *Foreign Affairs* 49 (January 1971): 218–36.

Kintner, William R. "Namibia: An Alternative Solution." *International Security Review* 6 (Winter 1981-1982): 533–52.

Liebenow, J. Gus. "American Policy in Africa: The Reagan Years." *Current History* 82 (March 1983): 97.

Lucius, Robert von and Totemeyer, Gerhard. "Namibia—A Regional Conflict and a World Problem." *Aussenpolitik* 30 (1979): 73–87.

Melber, Henning. "The National Union of Namibian Workers: Background and Formation." *Journal of Modern African Studies* 21 (March 1983): 151–58.

Monroe, Malcolm W. "Namibia—The Quest for The Legal Status of a Mandate: An Impossible Dream?" *International Lawyer* 5 (July 1971): 549–57.

Muhlemann, Christoph. "South West Africa: A Race Against Time." *Swiss Review of World Affairs* 26 (February 1977): 6–11.

"Namibia, South Africa, and the Walvis Bay Dispute." *Yale Law Review* 89 (April 1980): 903–22.

"Namibia—South Africa's Presence Found to Be Illegal—United Nations' Measures Declared Valid." *New York University Journal of International Law and Politics* 5 (Spring 1972): 117–38.

"Namibia." *UN Chronicle* 20 (December 1983): 4–14.

Nelson, Edward I. "Namibia: South African Puppet or Model for a Contingent?" *Western Goals Report* 2 (Spring 1984): 4–6.

"Nicaragua and Namibia Dominate Council Schedule." *UN Chronicle* 20 (July 1983): 34.

Nicol, Davidson. "United States Foreign Policy in Southern Africa: Third-World Perspectives." *Journal of Modern African Studies* 21 (December 1983): 587–603.

North, James. "Namibian Nightmare." *New Republic* 190 (February 13, 1984): 16–18.

O'Meara, Patrick. "South Africa: No New Political Dispensation." *Current History* 83 (March 1984): 105.

Ottaway, David. "Africa: U.S. Policy Eclipse." *Foreign Affairs* 58 (1979): 637–58.

Persaud, Motee. "Namibia and the International Court of Justice." *Current History* 68 (May 1975): 220–25.

Pollock, Alexander J. "The South West Africa Cases and the Jurisprudence of International Law." *International Organization* 23 (Autumn 1969): 767–87.

Pomerance, Michla. "The Admission of Judges Ad Hoc in Advisory Proceedings: Some Reflections in the Light of the Namibia Case." *American Journal of International Law* 67 (July 1973): 446–64.

Potts, James. "Angola and the U.S.: The Shape of a Prudent Compromise." *Backgrounder* 347 (1984): 10 p.

Richardson, Henry J., III. "Constitutive Questions in the Negotiations for Namibian Independence." *American Journal of International Law* 78 (January 1984): 76–120.

Rogers, Barbara. "Namibia: Test Case for the UN." *Vista* 8 (July-August 1972): 33.

Ropp, Klaus, Baron Von der. "Conflicts in Countries Surrounding South Africa." *Aussenpolitik* 34 (1983): 76–89.

———. "Hot Spots New and Old in Southern Africa." *Aussenpolitik* 31 (January 1980): 99–115.

———. "A New Era for Southern Africa?" *Aussenpolitik* 32 (1981): 297–310.

———. "South and South-West Africa/Namibia: At the Crossroads?" *Aussenpolitik* 34 (1983): 302–10.

Rotberg, Robert I. "The New Namibia." *Washington Quarterly* 1 (Autumn 1978): 13–25.

Rovine, Arthur W. and D'Amato, Anthony A. "Written Statement of the International League for the Rights of Man Filed With the International

Court of Justice in the Namibia Question." *New York University Journal of International Law and Politics* 4 (Summer 1971): 335–402.

"S.W. Africa Opinion of the I.C.J.: A Symposium (Part I)." *Columbia Journal of Transnational Law 11* (Winter 1972): 1–73.

"S.W. Africa Opinion of the I.C.J.: A Symposium (Part II)." *Columbia Journal of Transnational Law* 11 (Spring 1972): 193–239.

Samuels, Michael A. "U.S.-South African Relations Now." *Freedom at Issue* 67 (July-August 1982): 16–19.

Schermers, H. G. "The Namibia Decree in National Courts." *International and Comparative Law Quarterly* 26 (January 1977): 81–96.

Schweitzer, Thomas A. "The United Nations as a Source of Domestic Law: Can Security Council Resolutions be Enforced in American Courts?" *Yale Studies in World Public Order* 4 (Spring 1978): 162–273.

Seiler, John. "Policy Options in Namibia." *Africa Report* 29 (March-April 1984): 61–63.

———. "South Africa in Namibia: Persistence, Misperception, and Ultimate Failure." *Journal of Modern African Studies* 20 (December 1982): 689–712.

Shipley, Carl. "Namibia's Military, Economic and Political Importance to the U.S." *Lincoln Review* 4 (Fall 1983): 29–37.

Shultz, George P. "The U.S. and Africa in the 1980's."*Department of State Bulletin* 84 (April 1984): 9–12.

Sidler, Peter. "In a Peaceful Strip of Namibia."*Swiss Review of World Affairs* 33 (September 1983): 29.

Sigmon, Jan Alison. "Dispute Resolution in the United Nations: An Inefficient Forum?" *Brooklyn Journal of International Law* 10 (Summer 1984): 437–64.

Singham, A. W. "Namibia and Nuclear Proliferation." *Third World Quarterly* 3 (April 1981): 277–86.

———. "Namibia: Politics of Postponement." *Mainstream* (India) (December 8, 1984): 9.

Smith, Patrick L. "Namibia: The Pretense of Concern."*Nation* 223 (November 13, 1976): 493–98.

Somerville, Keith. "The U.S.S.R. and Southern Africa Since 1976." *Journal of Modern African Studies* 22 (March 1984): 73–108.

"South West Africa." *Africa Institute Bulletin* 7 (May 1969): 144–55.

"South West Africa." *Africa Institute Bulletin* 8 (April 1970): 121–30.

"South West Africa: Recent Political and Economic Developments." *Africa Institute Bulletin* 13 (July 1975): 155–64.

"Special Committee on Decolonization." *UN Monthly Chronicle* 8 (August-September 1971): 19–45.

Spence, J. E. "South Africa Between Reform and Retrenchment." *World Today* 40 (November 1984): 471–80.

————. "South Africa: Reform Versus Reaction."*World Today* 37 (December 1981): 461–68.

————. "South African Foreign Policy: Changing Perspectives." *World Today* 34 (November 1978): 417–25.

Spicer, Michael. "Namibia-Elusive Independence." *World Today* 36 (October 1980): 406–14.

Streek, Barry. "South Africa's Stake in the Border War."*Africa Report* 29 (March-April 1984): 57–60.

Stultz, Newell M. "Bridging the Black-White Gulf in Africa." *Orbis* 25 (Winter 1982): 881–902.

Suzuki, Eisuke. "Self-Determination and World Public Order: Community Response to Territorial Separation." *Virginia Journal of International Law* 16 (Summer 1976): 779–862.

Tauber, Laurence. "Legal Pitfalls of the Road to Namibian Independence." *Journal of International Law and Politics* 12 (Fall 1979): 375–410.

Thompson, W. Scott. "U.S. Policy Toward Africa: At America's Service?" *Orbis* 25 (Winter 1982): 1011–24.

Toler, Deborah. "Constructive Engagement: Reactionary Pragmatism at Its Best." *Issue: A Journal of Africanist Opinion* 12 (Fall-Winter 1982): 11–18.

Umozurike, U. O. "International Law and Self-Determination in Namibia." *Journal of Modern African Studies* 8 (December 1970): 585–603.

Ungar, Sanford J. "The Last Buffer." *Atlantic Monthly* 251 (June 1983): 24.

"The United Nations and Namibia." *Current World Leaders* 26 (December 1983): 895–912.

"U.S. Policy Toward Sub-Saharan Africa."*Orbis* 25 (Winter 1982).

"United States Policy Towards Africa: An A.S.A. Roundtable."*Issue: A Journal of Africanist Opinion* 12 (Fall- Winter 1982): 19–26.

Uttley, Garrick. "Globalism or Regionalism? United States Policy Towards Southern Africa." *Adelphi Papers* 154 (1979): 36 p.

Whitaker, Jennifer Seymour. "Africa Beset." *Foreign Affairs* 62 (1984): 746–76.

Wiechers, Marinus. "South West Africa and the World Court." *Bulletin of the Africa Institute of South Africa* 9 (November-December 1971): 449–61.

Woldring, Klaas. "Namibia: Reflections on Alternative Plans for Independence."*Australian Outlook* 35 (December 1981): 295–306.

Wolpe, Howard. "Africa and the U.S. House of Representatives." *Africa Report* 29 (July-August 1984): 67–71.

Zuijdwijk, Anthony J. M. "The International Court and South West Africa: Latest Phase." *Georgia Journal of International and Comparative Law* 3 (1973): 323–43.